Life Lessons, Observations, and Musings of An Elder

MIKE KEEBAUGH

PART I:
AUTHOR'S INTRODUCTION

Greetings from Geezerville

Geezerville is the geographic grouping of Sarasota, Florida and her eight barrier islands – home to retirees, snowbirds, and other seniors (the Chamber of Commerce seriously frowns upon using the term "old people"). Because geography is a science with two branches, physical and human, let me describe Geezerville in both aspects. Physically, Geezerville is located on the west coast of Florida (Gulf of Mexico) between Tampa Bay to the north and Naples to the south. In terms of human geography, Geezerville is somewhere between retirement and internment. Geezerville seduces seniors with its fine white-sand beaches, resorts, world-class medical facilities, cultural amenities, lack of a state income tax, and a wealth of restaurants. The area is a Pensioner's Paradise.

My wife, Andrée, and I live on the island of Longboat Key, which is known as Old Geezerville, not because it was established first, but rather because the median age on the island is 71. For the non-mathematicians out there in Readerland, that means half of the population is over

71 years old. The only place with older demographics is a cemetery.

In terms of senior citizens, Geezerville is the mecca of inactivity. So, all you Geezerites, get out there and wave those giant Styrofoam "We're Number One" fingers, or more appropriately, wave the "We're Number" fingers denoting that our physical and mental capabilities are numbing with age.

Welcome to my world. I am a 74-year-old retired defense company executive who has seen a lot over my life and career and seeks to share this experiential knowledge in humorous Life Lessons. I will delve deeper into Geezerville, retirement, aging and other life topics throughout the book.

Now sit back, and I hope you enjoy the ride. For you connoisseurs out there in Readerland, the suggested wine pairing for the book is a Cabernet Sauvignon.

Thanks to the Readers

If you bought this book, I want to thank you for contributing to my son's, granddaughter's, and "maverick" grandson's inheritance, as well as to several favorite charities that are in the will.

My son is a lawyer. (My wife and I are still lighting candles for him and trying to figure out where we went wrong. Oy Vey! – Yiddish for "Mamma Mia.") However, at least he is corporate counsel for a strategic consulting company, which ranks him above ambulance chaser, realtor, and used-car salesman on the Sleazy 100 Careers List.

My granddaughter is a precocious teenager who tackles everything with vigor and confidence. Apparently, she inherited a bunch of those female royal, Queenie genes from my wife, the Queen, who I will attempt to explain in time.

And I mention my "maverick" grandson since he has chosen to break tradition with the family's accepted, long-standing practices. Let me explain: (a) my wife, son, brother, sister-in-law, and I all went to Penn State; (b) my grandson was accepted at Penn State; and (c) my grandson is enrolled at Clemson. Mon Dieu! (which is French for OY Vey!!!) The British equivalent of this is Prince Harry leaving the royal family (I have empathy for Queen Elizabeth). He is still my favorite grandson, primarily because I only have one, but still....

If you bought this book on Kindle or Nook (you geeky high-techer, you!), bring it in to a book signing, and I'll write on the back of the device in Magic Marker.

If you borrowed this book from a library (yes, Virginia, libraries still exist in Middle America), I graciously hope you enjoy it. But please do me a favor and read it multiple times so others can't find it on the shelves and have to go out and buy it.

Why Am I Writing This Book?

I am 74 years old, and I have lived in a period of accelerating change. I now have the time to look back and reflect on all this, and I'd like to pass on some of what I have learned. Sound reasonable?

Hey, I'm just messing with you! Well it does sound good, and it rates a "Partial Truthiness" score if you measure me by the newspapers' Politifact Test (fact-check test for politicians) which asks, "Is John Doe Telling the Truth When He Says...?" By the way, "Partial Truthiness" is the highest rating that I have ever seen politicians achieve. Most of the time, they garner a capital "FALSE" score, which is commonly labeled "Liar, Liar, Pants on Fire!"

But let's get back to "why." I do believe I have learned some Life Lessons, and I will share them with you. The Life Lessons are presented as aphorisms. Did I just hear a big "HUH" out there in Readerland? Relax, Kemosabe. An aphorism is merely a statement of truth or opinion expressed in a concise, pithy, and witty manner, e.g., "A penny saved is a penny earned" or "If it ain't broke, don't fix it" (which, incidentally, we engineers believe should be "If it ain't broke, improve it").

Benjamin (Uncle Ben) Franklin is often credited as being the father of American aphorisms in his yearly *Poor Richard's Almanac*. It's a little-known fact that

Ben's common-law wife, Deborah Read, actually coined a number of these sayings for Benny, like "Early to bed, early to rise, makes a man healthy, wealthy, and boring" and "Go fly a kite, Ben." But there I go, off meandering and "embellishing the truth" once again.

There are two types of Life Lessons that I have documented:

1. In some cases, the lessons are derived from familiar quotes, parables, or sayings that aren't exactly accurate for the advice that I want to give, so I have improved, or "noodled," them to fit.

2. In the remaining cases, the lessons are conclusions that I have drawn, or more accurately "doodled," from my experiences.

So prepare to be noodled and doodled.

In this book, Life Lessons are like pimples. They are primarily concentrated in one place. (For pimples, it is usually on the face; in the book, it is in PART III, which is LIFE LESSONS.) However, have that Clearasil handy, they might pop up anywhere.

But the primary, driving reasons for writing this book are:

1. I have never written a book. It is on my bucket list, along with running with the bulls in Pamplona, attending a Rolling Stones concert before Sir Mick reaches 100, and going to a Hooters. And it's far, far safer than these examples. The bulls, the rockin' septuagenarians, and the young

Hooterettes are wild and crazy animals. For the curious readers, I discuss my bucket list in greater detail later in the book, so stand by.

2. Over the last eleven years, my wife and I have enjoyed extensive travel, and I have chronicled our adventures in a series of blogs which have resulted in feedback that was positive, e.g., "you are flat-ass funny and should write a book" (Texas friends), "you write like Dave Barry" (more on Dave later), and "I never knew that you had a sense of humor" (my former secretary).

3. I am a closet comedian. I love to tell stories and make people laugh. This is my attempt to come out of the closet. Peek-a-boo!

4. Time is not on my side. Consider the song "My Way." If you are a member of the Silent Generation, it was sung by Frank Sinatra. We Baby Boomers heard it from Elvis. Who the hell is singing it today, and is it rap? But I digress. The lyrics for "My Way" make my point. Just look at the opening line:

**"And now, the end is near
And so I face the final curtain."**

Hold on there for a minute, Grim Reaper! Not so fast!
I'm not planning on checking out anytime soon, but if life is a game, I'm in the fourth quarter. Nevertheless, I'm planning on several overtime periods. And it ain't

"sudden death" like hockey or soccer overtime; it's real overtime periods like basketball.

Anyhow, my message is contained in Life Lesson 1.

Life Lesson 1: If you want to do something, do it! You may not get another chance.

I have seen too many coulda/woulda/shouldas to wait. You have to play to win (coincidentally, the Pennsylvania Lottery theme). Just do it (Nike slogan). Buckle up, Buttercup ("Damn the torpedoes – full speed ahead" as Admiral "Daring Davey" Farragut proclaimed in the Battle of Mobile Bay)!

By the way, they say, "Opportunity knocks but once." I thought that I had heard it one time, but it was just the Amazon delivery man.

And just who is this person or group "They"? "They," the anonymous know-it-alls (according to the blogger Amy Claire[ii]), sure say a lot and get credit for being the purveyors of knowledge, and everyone accepts what "They" say as the gospel. But why?

Life Lesson 2 challenges this with an advertising-like jingle.

Life Lesson 2: Naysay "They say."

When someone says, "They say," be skeptical and don't accept it as a matter of fact. Ask who is "they" and how do you know it's true? It will probably quiet their bravado. At the very least, it should generate a pained facial expression and a few "humma, humma, hummas."

My advice is to be wary of groupthink. I have captured this in Life Lesson 3.

Life Lesson 3: Be careful when following the masses. Sometimes the "m" is silent.

The Title of This Book

If you google "How important is the title when selecting a book to read?" you will find unanimity among authors, editors, publishers, and bloggers. The answer is "damned significant." This gives us Life Lesson 4.

Life Lesson 4: You can judge a book by its title.

Now here's an example of a well-known proverb (You can't judge a book by its cover) that has been noodled to fit the situation.

The original title of this book was "Ramblings, Rantings, and Ravings of An Old Man." But my publicist said, "No friggin way, Grasshopper. You gotta have something sophisticated. Your own mother wouldn't buy it." And *The Old Man and the Sea* was already taken by a guy named Ernie Something.

Although I think my original title still has charisma, I deferred to her experience. And yet I wonder, WWDBD – What Would Dave Barry Do?

Anyhow, we compromised on "Life Lessons, Observations, and Musings of An Elder." Talk about sophistication? Whoo-eee! It just oozes with savoir faire (literally pixie dust).

Let's dissect the title.

I have already discussed Life Lessons above. They are "noodled" and "doodled" phrases that convey knowledge from my experiences, and they cover a wide range of topics to include writing a book, marriage, life with my wife the Queen, careers, Geezerville, retirement, neighbors and friends, aging, and travel.

Observations are oddities that I have noted along the journey, and you all know who you are. [Note to Editor – strike the last part of this sentence – End Note] My observations address changes I have noted over my lifetime, my picks for best and worst inventions, buggy whips created by inventions, politics, and the 5/95 Rule for Population Segmentation.

Musings are periods of reflection, introspection, or thought, e.g., "If a bullfrog had wings, he wouldn't go around bumping his ass on the ground all day." OK, maybe I need a better example. Basically, in Musings, my mind wanders freely, and sometimes aimlessly, through hobbies, music, my bucket list, offspring, and giving back.

How about "Elder"? The noun "elder" has three definitions: (1) an aged person, often a wise aged person; (2) an officer of a religious group; and (3) a tree or a bush. I am certain that I am one of the three, having experienced over 27,000 days on this Earth.

In many cultures, elders are repositories of knowledge, gained from many years of living, who transmit this information as story tellers, advisors, and mentors. My intent is to share my experiences and advice in an amusing and playful way. Peek-a-boo! Closet comedian here. I want the reader to enjoy the ride.

So, convinced that I can compete in the market where old guys are passing along wisdom, I strike out on my journey with confidence and Life Lesson 5.

Life Lesson 5: You eliminate your competition by outliving the bastards.

This is a good Plan A, and if it doesn't work, you don't need a Plan B.

Think about it.

Disclosures

In the name of fairness and political correctness, I find it necessary to disclose several items about this book.

Actually, it really has nothing to do with fairness, etc. My lawyer demands that I disclose them. I have a litigious bunch of colleagues (translated as "group of sue-crazy SOBs") who are mentioned in the book. They would like nothing more than to sue me if they thought there was money to be made.

Disclosure 1. Joe Friday almost got it right on *Dragnet* when he said, "The names have been changed to protect the innocent." In this book, when describing people, the names have been changed to protect my butt.

Disclosure 2. Parts of this book are true; parts

are not (they are what we authors call "embellished"). The problem is that I can't remember which is which. So the reader is left to figure it out – think of it as homework.

Disclosure 3. I originally wrote this book under the nom de plume – pen name for you non-Francophiles out there in Readerland – of Mark Twain, but my lawyer felt that 70% of my readers would know that he is dead. So, after considerable thought, this book was written under the pen name of "Samuel Clemens."

Disclosure 4. My favorite two humor writers, excluding politicians and newspapers (which are both hilariously funny), are Mark Twain and Dave Barry. I also enjoy Carl Hiaasen, even though he writes some weird stuff about Florida – but then again, Florida is weird – and Jason Gay, a columnist for the *Wall Street Journal* who primarily writes about sports and The Grumpy Old Lobster Boat Captain, Bill Belichick.

Why do I keep sucking up to Dave Barry? He is a funny, funny, funny individual who was a columnist for the *Miami Herald* until 2005 and is now an author of books on life, a blogger, and a special events columnist. He is famous, and did I mention funny? He is well known as an author. His books sell. My premise is that if I am complimentary to him, he might read my book and mention it in his writings. He might even give me an endorsement for my jacket notes under "What other authors are saying about this book."

[Note to Dave – I have drafted a quick endorsement for you if you are too busy to read the book:

***"Life Lessons, Observations and Musings of An Elder* is brilliant and funny. Buy this book."**

By the way, Dave, if you can't do this, I understand. I realize you are extremely busy with the rock band, the writing, and living in the Witness Protection Program after your narrow escape from Miami. Don't worry. I'll get Mark to do it. Thanks, Dave. – End Note]

Book Rating

In compliance with the Motionless Picture Association of America, this book is rated CG-13, which means children are strongly cautioned that some material may not be appropriate for parents. At the very least, parents may have to ask their thirteen-year-old children to explain phrases.

In the book, I have attempted to limit my use of four-letter words to "shit" and "ass." OK, "ass" is technically not a four-letter word, but it is the past pluperfect tense of "shithole." Anyhow, these two words and their derivations, e.g., shit-faced, shithead, asshole, etc., may appear in the book. If you find this offensive, you can call 1-800-PURITAN and order the Saint edition of the book (for a nominal additional charge) which has "s" replaced by "$" and "i" replaced by "*," yielding "$h*t" and "a$$." Then you won't have to hide the book in your underwear drawer when the cleaning lady comes. Peace of mind for a few pennies more.

Let's now move on to PART II, which is THE PRO-CESS, with a reminder from Bill Murray to keep us grounded.

Life Lesson 6: Life is not a fairy tale. If you lose your shoes at midnight, Cinderella, you are drunk!

Sobering thought? Nah! Lighten up and enjoy.

PART II: THE PROCESS

Chapter 1:
Getting Started

I have made "The Commitment" – I am going to write a book. Now I face the challenging task of figuring out the correct book genre (French for gender – don't they ever think of anything but sex?). To an author, genre means a specific type of writing, and it is important in making sure the book is categorized properly to match the potential audience. I know you're thinking "child's play," but not so fast, Mr. Uninitiated. My book is mostly nonfiction (except for an occasional embellishment here and there – OK, maybe more frequently). However, according to Mark Malatesta's *Book Genre Dictionary*,[ii] there are 82 genres within Nonfiction.

I initially believed that I was writing a memoir. I should point out that a memoir is different from an autobiography. An autobiography is the story of one's life – ashes to ashes, and more than you want to know. A memoir, hopefully, leaves out the boring parts (and the incarcerations, wild parties, children out of wedlock, etc. – just kidding!!!).

However, memoir doesn't really capture the book. Yes, it is part memoir, and it is also part self-improvement, and part general nonfiction. But the overriding theme (if I can pull it off) is humor. In the book, I use a series of vignettes or descriptions of experiences to tell my story and share advice in an entertaining and playful way that leads to lessons and observations. It is primarily intended to amuse the readers and make them laugh.

Vignette – Friends, here is a word that is worth the price of the book alone. Say it loud! Say it proud! Vignette. Vignette. Vignette. You are sounding so erudite. For your edification (there I did it again –– another freebie meaning "intellectual improvement"), I plan to introduce these free vocabulary-enrichment terms as appropriate throughout the book. You too can become a silver-tongued televangelist, politician, or college professor (all at no additional cost).

Now that I know what I am writing and why, I said to myself, "Mike (which is what I call me when I talk to myself), are you ready? Let's write a nonfiction humor book with multiple subgenres."

Do you hear a big gulp here? **[Note to Publicist – Investigate the potential for 7-Eleven sponsorship if we capitalize "Big Gulp." And while you are at it, look at lining up sponsors like NASCAR does, e.g., we could wear the sponsors' logos on our leisure suits at book signings, TV promo tours, etc. – End Note]**

The question is "How do I get started?"

Fortunately, today's author has the internet, Google, and Amazon. Suddenly I'm feeling sorry for Mark Twain, who lacked these resources and had only his corncob pipe and bushy eyebrows to rely on.

So Step 1 was to search "How to write a humor book" in both Amazon and Amazon Kindle books.

Amazon Kindle lists over 1,275 results and Amazon

has 400. They range from *The Complete Idiot's Guide to Comedy Writing* on the low end to *The Art of Comedy Writing* on the genteel end.

In the words of Gomer Pyle – Golly! Surprise, surprise, surprise!

The books' titles promise you can write a book in 3, 4, 7, 8, 10, 11, or 13 steps. Some claim that you will be able to write your book in 10 minutes a day (although the number of days required is not given), or 45 hours, or 30 to 40 days.

Other Kindle and Amazon descriptors include "practical guide" (who wants an impractical guide?), "simple," "write good" (I swear), "make money," "write quickly," "graphic memoirs" (now we're talking), and "style" (gimme some of that). Did I mention "make money"?

The prices of the books ranged from a low of free (e.g., *How to Write Funny*) to a high of $112.00.

To show my hipness – I'm sure that is still a cool word – I checked out YouTube and discovered more than 400 how-to videos and articles. Confusion rules.

My bottom line to this investigation was that there is no consensus on how to write a book, and opinions are extensive. I can state this simply as Life Lesson 7.

Life Lesson 7: All authors have two things in common: opinions and assholes, and hopefully the former fits into the latter.

When it comes to how to write, you are entitled to your own opinion (or opinions) – join the crowd of authors and express yourself in a manner and a process that are comfortable to you.

Plan B

Given this initial setback, I asked myself "Mike, WWDBD (What Would Dave Barry Do)?" The answer was simple. I had a couple of beers.

Then I decided to set out on my own, in the true American spirit, like our forefathers and our foremothers. Heading west in my Conestoga wagon named MacBook Pro, accompanied by my guides Mr. Google and Lady YouTube. The John Wayne of the 21st century. Wagons Ho, pilgrim!

Progress

How am I doing with respect to time? My research assistant (Mr. Google) found that the average book is 90,000 to 100,000 words, and the average teen book is 55,000 words. This raises a question in my mind. Is it because teens can't focus for 100,000 words? Also, show me a teen who reads books. They are glued to their phones. But again, I digress. The average nonfiction book is 70,000 words. To date, I have drafted less than 2,900 words in 25 days. If I add editing and rewrites to this, I'm on pace to finish in 2.5 years. This is so disheartening that I think I'll take a wine break.

OK. I'm back!

I just had a Wine Flash! You might know it as a light-bulb moment or an Aha! moment. It's when you recognize something that might make a difference. Here it is:

While the average memoir is 75,000 words, the average self-help book is 40,000 words. And since I'm writing a self-help memoir, which is a new literary subgenre I created, I can arbitrarily set the ideal length at around 55,000 words, which is almost halfway between the two. Therefore, at my pace, I will finish in 1.9 years.

Whew! I feel better already.

Chapter 2:
Tax Considerations

One of my first research projects in writing the memoir was to find out what tax deductions I might claim.[iii] Pay dirt, baby! Cha-ching! Cha-ching! Let me educate you.

The IRS is pseudo-friendly to writers, which is as friendly as they get. One way is permitting deductions for producing manuscripts. Is this a great country or what? Some of the biggies are:

1. Equipment – I plan to include my purchases of a new computer, two printers, two desks, two ergonomic chairs (I have two homes and can't drag printers, desks, and chairs between them, now can I?), software, wine (more details later under Writing Regime), paper, and "supplies," which is a vague aggregate that I expect to be of significant value, with a capital "SIGNIFICANT."

2. Self-employment tax – One can deduct half of self-employment taxes.

3. Office Space – Clearly, I have two homes, which means two home offices, which means two deductions. QED, or Quod Erat Demonstrandum, which is Latin for "There's the proof, baby – deduct, deduct, deduct."

4. Health Insurance – One can deduct 100% of all premiums.

5. Hired Help – Of course, I will deduct editors, proofreaders, office cleaners, and my costs for looking good at book signings, e.g., barber, tailor, etc., and I will require at least one personal assistant to handle fan mail and email.

6. Travel – Research is essential. In the past eleven years, my wife and I have traveled around the globe on what we mistakenly called vacations. It turns out that these trips were actually research for memoir adventure events included in the book. **[Note to CPA – How do I claim these expenses retroactively? – End Note]**

7. Meals – A writer has to eat! I plan to deduct part of the meal costs for dinner meetings with my wife (strike that – I mean personal assistant) to discuss reader relations.

8. Conferences – One must mingle with people in the trade to maximize visibility and become part of "The Writers' Club." I plan to ask Dave Barry for a list of recommended conferences that are held in warm, exotic get-away places.

9. Vehicle Expenses – This seems ripe for the picking. I believe that to create an image, an author should drive something foreign and fast such as a Maserati or a Porsche. Face it. No one is going to remember you if you show up for a book signing in a Prius.

What I have discovered is summed up in Life Lesson 8.

Life Lesson 8: Render unto Caesar the things that are Caesar's, but look for loopholes.

Always remember: interpretation of the allowable deductions is an art, not a science.

Also keep in mind what Dave Barry cautioned: "We try to cooperate fully with the IRS because, as citizens, we feel a strong patriotic duty not to go to jail."

I started this chapter by discussing my commitment to write a humorous book. Easy said, Captain Novice. If you are not careful, there are some pitfalls which can grab you by the tooties and shipwreck you, derail you, or just plain bite you in the ass. Let's look at two of them: procrastination and writer's block.

Chapter 3: Procrastination

Procrastination is best summarized by Life Lesson 9.

Life Lesson 9: Saying is easy. Doing is not.

Or as the Brits might say, stating your intent is a "piece of piss," which means "easy." Colorful folks, those Brits.

Face it, writing is something new and unfamiliar to a beginning author. It is tempting to avoid putting pen to paper (or fingers to keyboard for you techies). There is always some fishing show on TV that you would rather watch.

I think Mae West, the noted 20th-century philosopher and sex symbol, provided the best advice on procrastination, so I will repeat her words as Life Lesson 10.

Life Lesson 10: He who hesitates is last.

Once a commitment is made, it important to get on with it; however, I have two caveats about procrastination that seniors should consider.

The first is Life Lesson 11.

Life Lesson 11: Old people should procrastinate. Maybe they won't have to do it.

And the second, Life Lesson 12, is an old pilots' saying.

Life Lesson 12: It's better to be late than "the late."

Think about it.

Chapter 4:
Writing Regime

I know most authors will tell you that one of the most difficult parts to writing is "writer's block," aka brain freeze. It's kinda like constipation of the mind. Listen up, kiddies –– I think I have discovered a foolproof way to get around writer's block. My writing regime is as follows:

1. As a first step, I put my ideas together on potential topics and points that I want to make. This can be done at any time of the day and over a period of multiple days, not months, you procrastinators. (Did you skip the previous section?)

2. Next, I begin each morning by reviewing the topics, organizing them into chapters, and annotating the outline.

3. Then I put it away and enjoy the day. A nap or two can't hurt, but keep a pen and paper (or iPhone) ready at all times to capture that flash of brilliance that may strike you. Do not – I repeat, do not – trust your questionable memory!

4. Then in the evening, following dinner, I retreat to my minimally furnished office (the IRS may be reading along) with a bottle of red wine and

begin putting my thoughts on paper. I write like Hemingway until the wine is gone.

5. The red wine is a stimulant. I have not been faced with writer's block since I started this practice. The words flow like the wine flows – fast and sensuous.

   However, there is one caution to this process: I admit that sometimes the next morning, I have real trouble deciphering what I wrote the night before. The hazards of being an author!

6. Now I repeat Steps 1 through 5, and repeat, and repeat... until I'm satisfied with the material. Then I turn it over to my editor, the Queen, for critical suggestions. This usually results in a difference of opinions, better known as a shouting match.

I encourage wannabe writers to try out the regime. The worst case is that you spend your evenings secluded in your writer's cave, away from your spouse's blaring TV tuned to the Cooking Channel (more on this later), drinking wine.

By the way, I'm already considering my next book: *How to Write a Best Seller While Half in The Bag.*

So now I hope you understand why I will be claiming cases of wine as a tax write-off. It's a necessary part of the process. Remember Life Lesson 13.

Life Lesson 13: Wine is the answer. What's the problem?

Wine (yes, dear, I'll add "in measured quantities") can help solve a variety of shortcomings. For example, if you're shy, it cures introvertiveness (I may have just coined a word). If you have two left feet, it will make you dance (maybe not well, but you'll be out on the floor). If you're quiet, Hello, Mr. Pontificator! And if you are on hold, listening to elevator music and waiting for a customer service agent, it will help pass the 90-minute delay. (P.S. it will also help you understand what the agent is saying in a foreign accent once you are finally connected.) Wine is the closest thing to a panacea that I have found.

Louis "Sterile Louie" Pasteur weighed in to support wine as a creative tool when he said: "A bottle of wine contains more philosophy than all the books in the world."

And one additional note about the benefits of imbibing. Most discussions focus on people dying because of alcohol. Do you realize how many people are born because of it?

Chapter 5:
Assistance and Environment

My Assistant, Mr. Google

The smartest "person" on the planet is not Donald Trump (sorry, Big Guy), or Albert Einstein, or any living human being. The smartest person on the earth is Mr. Google. He knows everything about anything and recalls it quickly and vividly. I am pleased to have Mr. Google as my research assistant. By the way, he works cheap. I have provided more details about this genius in Best Inventions when I discuss Musings later.

[Note to Reader – There is controversy on my team about naming Mr. Google as the "smartest person on the planet." My agent, personal assistant and editor (aka my wife) believes it should be Ms. Google because "women are inherently smarter than men." The discussions continue. I'm stalling while I search for counterarguments. Meanwhile, I'm making my own meals, doing my laundry, and living in silence – End Note]

A Final Note on my Writing Environment

I have one – make that two – little challenges that I face in writing a book. They are Essential Tremor (ET) and Parkinson's Disease (PD).

Essential tremor (ET)[iv] is a neurological disorder

that causes involuntary and rhythmic shaking. It can affect almost any part of your body, but the trembling occurs most often in the hands – especially when doing simple tasks such as drinking from a glass or tying shoelaces.

Essential tremor is usually not a dangerous condition, but it typically worsens over time and can be severe in some people. I was diagnosed with ET six years ago and have been on medication to ameliorate the tremors since then.

Parkinson's Disease (PD)[v] is a long-term degenerative disorder of the central nervous system that mainly affects the motor system. As the disease worsens, non-motor symptoms become more common. Early in the disease, the most obvious symptoms are shaking, rigidity, slowness of movement, and difficulty with walking. The cause of Parkinson's Disease is unknown, but it is believed to involve both genetic and environmental factors. The motor symptoms of the disease arise from the death of cells in the midbrain. This results in not enough dopamine in this region of the brain.

There is no cure for Parkinson's Disease. Treatment aims to improve the symptoms. As the disease progresses and neurons continue to be lost, these medications become less effective and produce involuntary writhing movements. I was diagnosed with Parkinson's five years ago.

The interesting thing is that only 5% of people diagnosed with ET also contract PD. I'm one of the few that got the double whammy. Maybe I should go out and buy a lottery ticket?

Now, this ain't no pity party. Each of us has our challenges, and you play the hand (albeit shaky) that you were dealt. The reason I mention it is that these two conditions make typing on a keyboard difficult, often resulting in two or three letters when a key is depressed. So, if youuu ssee sommethinggg like this, it'ss just a case where I have missed the corrections during editing.

One great aid in generating my initial draft was Apple's Voice Recognition. If you speak slowly, it does a reasonable job in translating to text, even with my Appalachian hillbilly accent, bastardized by fourteen years living in Texas.

There are some positives about having ET and PD:

1. I lost my sense of smell, so I can drink cheap wine and think it's good. You can also pass gas around me, and I won't know it.

2. I can make one hell of a martini (shaken, not stirred).

3. I've learned to play the castanets. **[Note to Dave Barry – If you and Stephen King are considering getting the band back together and you need a castanet player for The Rock Bottom Remainders, I'm your man. Call me. – End Note]**

Segue

Segue is an Italian word for "quit messing around and show me the beef," i.e., move on smoothly. In this case, we will move on to PART III, which is LIFE LESSONS.

PART III:
LIFE LESSONS

Chapter 6:
My Life (To Date)

No, this isn't an autobiography, but to put things in perspective, here's a synopsis of the first 74 years.

I grew up in McConnellsburg, a small farming community in south-central Pennsylvania. The population of the town was, and remains, around 1,200. We had a total of two traffic lights, and that was only because there was a BOGO offer – buy one, get one free. The town's big claim to fame was – wait a minute, I'm thinking – hmmm – I guess we didn't have one?

My parents owned and operated a propane gas and appliance store and a furniture store. So when I became old enough, I worked there on weekends, delivering 100-pound cylinders filled with liquid propane gas, appliances, and furniture. Given this valuable experience, I crossed it off the What I Want To Be When I Grow Up list.

I attended public school there, and my graduating class was 53 students. That was after we had merged with another school district. We weren't a one-room schoolhouse, but you could count the rooms on your fingers and toes.

I guess that I was the typical Baby Boomer teenager growing up in the '50s. Well, technically, I'm not a Baby Boomer. As my research assistant, Mr. Google, pointed out to me, a Baby Boomer was born between January 1946 and December 1964. My birth date is November 10, 1945, which misses the window by 51 days, but I figure when you are 74 years old, what the hell is 51 days? – it's a rounding error (.2%). So I am a pseudo Baby Boomer. Besides, who wants to be a member of the Silent Generation that preceded us cool Baby Boomers?

We spent most of our teenage years being cool, or at least thinking we were cool. We invented rock and roll, much to our parents' dismay. We enjoyed listening to Elvis Presley, that shameless, swivel-hipped, side-burned pagan. And every afternoon at three o'clock, we turned on the snowy black-and-white television to watch Dick Clark's *American Bandstand* – Wop Bop A Loo Bop A Lop Bam Boom! Just seeing Annette Funicello was worth the price of admission.

We also discovered transistor radios, which were the size of a shoebox, weighed 50 pounds, and held a dozen D-cell batteries – the original Walkman.

As teenage boys, there were two things on our minds – girls and cars.

Girls

In a town of 1,200 residents, there are a limited number of choices to date. Therefore, your intrepid, hormone-oozing boys traveled to the big city, Chambersburg, PA, population 20,000, "cruised" the streets, and attended all the dances, fairs, and carnivals to meet girls. Hey, what's

25 miles each way, traversing the Tuscarora Mountain, to a young driver paying 29 cents a gallon for gasoline? And these were some finely sophisticated girls who didn't chew gum every waking hour of the day. Love was in the air.

The accepted wisdom here is "The grass is always greener on the other side of the fence." In our case, it was a corollary, which is Life Lesson 14.

Life Lesson 14: The girls are always grander on the other side of the mountain.

Cars

Now, don't get me wrong. Girls may be fun, but a guy's real love was his car, no if's and's or but's! There are two kinds of people in this world – people who use cars to get from point A to point B, and CAR GUYS, whose cars are their mistresses (there may be a third kind out there who lives in the Himalayas or Lower Slobovia or other Godforsaken place and has never heard of a car, but they aren't relevant here). Speaking of relevancy, again I digress. My point is that I am a Car Guy, and so were all my friends growing up.

I started driving my father's trucks when I was twelve – working in his warehouse area, gassing them up, loading and unloading tanks and merchandise, etc.

Turning sixteen and getting a driver's license was magical. My parents gave me a 1939 Chevrolet four-door sedan – three-speed transmission and a GMC truck engine. And it had suicide doors, i.e., the rear doors were hinged at the rear rather than the front. I loved it. Joe Cool, Cool Hand Luke, and Fonzie rolled into one.

I spent hours tinkering with the Chevy – washing it, polishing it, waxing it, customizing it, punching out the muffler to get a deep throaty roar, etc. I also spent hours cruising the town with my friends and looking for whatever we looked for – it's been so long I forget. When we got tired of cruising or we got low on gas, we all gathered at the local ESSO station and "shot the shit."

Of course, we formed a car club, the McConnellsburg Road Aces, and we got a logo with four ace cards fanned out. We ordered front license plates and white jackets with our logo on them, and "We Looked Marvelous" as Billy Crystal used to say. Come to think of it, we really didn't do anything more as a club. Oh, well.

For some unknown reason, perhaps in celebration or maybe because of my weird sense of humor, at the end of my senior year in high school, I used white shoe polish to paint "cute little signs" on my car windows – like "Don't laugh, lady, your daughter may be in here" and "Christine Keeler slept here," etc. **[Note to Reader – For those of you who are too young to remember Christine Keeler, she was a model who was involved with an English government minister, John Profumo, in the early '60s. – End Note]**

Needless to say, this endeared me to the local community, who tittered, "That boy will never amount to nothing," "His parents are such nice people," and "Hell Raiser!"

This leads to Life Lesson 15.

Life Lesson 15: Some people can't take a joke.

Come to think of it, there is also Life Lesson 16.

Life Lesson 16: Cars are a lot like girls – they look good and they can take you where you want to go, but if you buy/marry one, you could be disappointed in the trade-in value.

College to Present

I attended Penn State and got my degree in mathematics. (I started in Engineering but couldn't see myself wearing a slide rule in a holster or using a pocket protector.) College was where we learned to smoke, drink, chase girls, gamble and, oh yeah, pursue knowledge. Today's high school students are already proficient at these pursuits, so they use college to further hone their skills. While at Penn State, I experienced two life changing events: (1) I met the Queen, my future wife, and (2) I began working part-time for a defense contractor, HRB Singer – a division of the Singer Sewing Machine company. You probably never realized that those sewing machine people were also intelligence spooks, did you?

Upon the Queen's graduation, we were married, and when I graduated, I went full time with HRB. I received a MS in Computer Science while working there. As for life with the Queen, I have devoted two chapters to her later in this book – and she is still lobbying for more.

During the 42 years of my career, I survived five mergers (four from the acquiree's side, not the acquirer – pucker-up time, over and over, to establish credentials).

This was the era of consolidation in the defense industry and is further discussed in Chapter 12. I advanced from software developer to project manager to Engineering VP to President of HRB to GM of a large Texas site of E-Systems to VP of Imagery and Geospatial Systems. My final position was as a Raytheon VP and President of Raytheon Intelligence and Information Systems.

I retired and we moved to the Sarasota, Florida area in 2009. We also have a fish camp in central Pennsylvania where I go to pursue the elusive trout in the spring and to escape the summer heat, humidity, and hurricanes in Florida.

The bottom line is that I have been very fortunate. I live in Paradise and I'm on the sunny side of the sod. The Queen and I have been married for 53 WONDERFUL years, a rarity today, where only 6% of all marriages last 50 years or more. In Chapter 11, I will elaborate on marriage and its Life Lessons.

OK. It's time for a reader check. If you made it so far, but just barely, tweet me at @HanginIn. If you are enjoying it, tweet me at @Peedmypants. If you already gave up, how are you reading this page?

Now let's take a look at the love of my life, the Queen. For reference, a queen is the female ruler of an independent state. In my case, the Queen rules the world.

A queen is also a woman who is important or successful at something, e.g., a queen of fashion. A queen is independent, strong-willed, social, demanding, and a teacher. She expects to be recognized as a queen. Did I marry the poster child for a queen or what? Let me describe.

Chapter 7:
The Queen-To-Be

The Queen-To-Be was born on Halloween (in an attempt to attain 54 WONDERFUL years of marriage, I'll gracefully refrain from any comments regarding coincidence) and raised in Beaver Falls, Pennsylvania, a steel town near the Ohio border. Rumor has it that in high school she dated Joe Willie Namath, but she vehemently denies it, saying he was much older than her (according to Wikipedia, only two years – hmmm). She also denies being Miss Beaver County 1962. Snopes is silent on both rumors. Only the Queen knows for sure.

Dating

I first met the Queen-To-Be during our freshman year at Penn State while walking to class, but she doesn't remember it. So much for first impressions, Romeo! What a ladykiller – fresh out of McConnellsburg High School, hair slicked back with Brylcreem, white socks and all. Get in line, girls!

Subsequently, I joined a fraternity, and I would see her at parties since, over the years, she dated almost all of my fraternity brothers. I guess I became the last man standing, so to speak.

We first got together while preparing for Spring Week. Spring Week was a carnival where fraternities and sororities paired up to put together a float for the Spring Week parade and to develop skits for carnival shows. In other words, one week of cutting classes, drinking beer and partying in the name of brotherhood/sisterhood. Everything was done under the auspices of a theme which changed each year, e.g., "For the Glory of Old State," "Chug-a-lug," "Toga," etc. The Queen-To-Be's sorority and my fraternity were partners during our junior year.

She and I seemed to enjoy our time together, so I decided to ask her out on a date. Let me set the stage. I was a serious (don't say "nerdy") student. In fact, the "B" I got in Bowling destroyed my GPA. I believed in being prepared and studied for tests well in advance. She was from the Socialize, Have Fun, and Cram The Night Before A Test discipline.

So I called her and asked if she would like to go on a date with me to Pattee Library to study for finals, which were two weeks away.

Her response was "Oh gee, that sounds like fun. I've never been in Pattee Library before." Did I mention we were juniors? The red warning lights should have been flashing and the DEFCON I sirens wailing! Never been in the library! Wonder where my fraternity brothers took her on dates? What was I thinking? Why didn't I run like hell?

P.S. We went on the date, and she wanted to talk the whole time, which was seriously frowned upon in the stacks. First time I was ever thrown out of a library. But it was kinda fun.

Shortly thereafter, our relationship almost ended when she found a pair of ladies' panties in the glove compartment of my car. To this day, I swear I don't know how they got there. Maybe my fraternity brothers were pulling a prank on me? (Help me out here readers. Give me some possibilities. Text me at "ASSINSLING" or 277-467-5464.) The worst part was that I had to wear them for a month to prove they were mine. Just kidding – it was only two weeks.

Oh yeah, I should probably mention that she was engaged to a local Beaver Falls boy at the time, though that didn't seem to influence our dating. I guess that creates Life Lesson 17.

Life Lesson 17: Absence makes the heart forget.

This may not be a universal truth, but it sure applied in our case.

Summer and Fall

The Queen-To-Be decided to go to summer school and advance a term to graduate early. Meanwhile, I got a job at HRB as a summer employee. The bottom line is that we were together during the summer and had a great time. In the fall we continued to date, and at Christmas I gave her a ring. (I think that according to Emily Post's Rules of Wedding Etiquette, she had to return the Beaver Falls guy's ring at that time?) We planned our wedding for her graduation day on March 25th.

We got married on the day before Easter. Our minister gave us a bottle of champagne to celebrate the occasion. We could only afford to go to Washington, DC on our honeymoon – I was a student, she was an unemployed graduate, and did I mention it was Easter? Not much was happening as we searched to find a place to eat, finally settling on a Howard Johnson's that was one of the few open restaurants. That night, we retreated to our room, opened the champagne, and turned on the TV. After one glass of champagne, the Queen-To-Be fell asleep, and I finished the bottle of champagne watching Johnny Carson reruns. This probably was a sign of things to come. We were young and broke, but we had a Corvette (details provided in an upcoming chapter).

Married Life

The Queen-To-Be took a job selling women's clothes in State College. I graduated with my bachelor's degree in Mathematics and began full-time employment at HRB. Very early in the marriage, the Queen-To-Be became pregnant and we had a son, Todd. I also pursued my MS in Computer Science during this period.

When we were first married, we could only afford to rent an old trailer at the Hilltop Trailer Park outside of State College. What a cramped engineering marvel. Each door served two purposes – in one direction it closed off Room A, and in the other direction, Room B. And the standard-size bed went wall to wall in the bedroom. We survived because my mother sent us a letter every day with two dollars enclosed, five dollars on Fridays. Loved to see that mailman coming. This worked OK until the Queen-To-Be began seeing snakes in our unmowed lawn. (Yes, mowing was my responsibility, and I blew it.) So the royal decision was issued – we are outta here!

It was late spring, and I accepted an offer to live in

my fraternity house and house-sit for the summer. The price was right. All I had to do was watch out for vandals, etc., and mow the lawn. Since I had previous experience mowing (well, I might have padded my resume a bit), I accepted. Life was good again – almost. What my fraternity advisor forgot to mention was that in the summer, the furnace was shut down, and yep, you guessed it – no hot water. So we sucked it up. I went to Rec Hall every morning to shower and shave for work. And every evening I heated water on the gas stove to fill the Queen-To-Be's bath. Is this marriage off to a good start or what? We learned two Life Lessons here.

Life Lesson 18: Beggars can't be choosers.

and

Life Lesson 19: TANSTAAFL (There ain't no such thing as a free lunch.)

After the summer of fun, we moved into a series of apartments and lived closer to how normal people do. We eventually scraped up enough down-payment money to purchase a home and began living the life of June and Ward Cleaver. The Queen-To-Be worked as an elementary teacher. Meanwhile, I pursued being a software weenie. Later, the Queen-To-Be changed careers and went into real estate. So eventually I had a son studying to become a lawyer and a wife in real estate – two of us on the Sleazy 100 Careers List.

Chapter 8:
The Metamorphosis

Enough history! How did the Queen-To-Be morph into the Queen? Please check the right answer:

A. Genetics – It's in the genes

B. Association with the wrong friends

C. Husband busy pursuing a career

D. She's a Scorpio

E. Damned if I know!

F. All of the above

Time's up. Pencils down. The correct answer is F, "All of the above."

Let's examine each of the factors.

First, her mother was a "ruling" queen who exercised control over her father. The scepter didn't fall too far from the tree. Wait a minute. I'm mixing metaphors. That is "apple," isn't it?

Second, she got in with a group who enjoyed the finer things of life and bought them. The two or three credit card offers in the mail each day didn't help matters.

Third, the situation lacked checks and balances. Since I was busy, I turned over all operating decisions and finances to her. Dumber than dirt!

Fourth, Scorpios exhibit passion and power, and she gets an A Plus Plus here.

And finally, as Flip Wilson used to say in his Geraldine character, "The devil made me do it." Old Satan got to her.

This evolution occurred over a period of years while she climbed the Queenie ladder.

The metamorphosis of a Queen-To-Be to a Queen is like a hurricane – it starts out as a small disturbance, and under the right conditions it can grow to a Category 5 storm, which has a powerful punch.

Chapter 9:
Division of Responsibilities

Any successful marriage (the definition of "successful" is left to the reader – I know some of you think "successful marriage" is an oxymoron) depends on a division of responsibilities. In our marriage:

1. The Queen is responsible for:

    a. The "Expenditure" side of the balance sheet – as those of you who took Accounting 101 know, this is where the money goes;
    b. Selections – Choosing clothing, wine, activities, friends, restaurants, etc. for both of us – if a choice is needed, she's The Man;
    c. "Joint" Family Decisions – Resolving where to live, where to vacation, if her mother should move in with us, etc.; and
    d. Deciding when I have to shave and what I should wear.

2. I am responsible for:

    a. The "Income" side of the balance sheet; and
    b. Carrying out the decisions of the Queen.

Once she had risen to the throne and attained royal status, the Queen developed certain expectations and standards to be met. Let's look at them.

Chapter 10:
Queenie Requirements

In Chapters 8 and 9, I described the evolution of the Queen and what it's like serving Her Majesty.

And yes, I own up to helping create her. Mea culpa (I am the culprit). Fifty lashes of the whip, you guilty peasant!

If you are dealing with a queen, it is critical that you understand her world – what is important and essential to her, her language, her God-given capabilities, her likes and her dislikes, and the royal standards. If you don't, you will become chopped liver. Remember, she is the Queen.

I have compiled a list that works for me. Hopefully you can use this to understand your Queen.

The Queen Today

I said that the Queen has evolved over a period of years.

Today, in her final incarnation, she sees the world as follows:

1. Her Expectations: "Acceptable" is a rating of Four Stars and above. Anything lower is entirely out of the question, and you will be verbally chastised if you have the gall to suggest it. What could you be thinking, knave?

She might even be capable of the "stink eye"; remember her birthday is Halloween!

2. Her Birthright Knowledge: She is the consummate professional counselor and advice-giver. This includes giving driving directions (step aside, GPS – the Queen knows a better way), psychiatric counseling (you have a problem, honey), diagnosing medical issues and suggesting treatments (Doctor Queenie), critic (perhaps her Numero Uno forte), coach (e.g., I don't need any golf lessons; she continually provides pointers when we play), back seat driver (I could drive with blinders on and follow her directions), and haberdasher (on my own, I could never select the proper attire). To hear her speak, she must have about 50 honorary PhDs from the best colleges in the nation.

The age-old saying "If you want something done right, do it yourself" doesn't quite hit the mark when it comes to the Queen, so I have refined it as follows:

Life Lesson 20: If you want something done right, ask the Queen for directions.

3. Her Mentoring Skills: She firmly believes that she made me successful. Obviously, I could not have done it on my own. I'd still be just a poor old country boy running his inherited furniture store in south-central Pennsylvania. Her mentoring follows the Success-Monetary System model which is "You have to be successful because I like expensive things."

4. The Socialite: She is a people person with many friends and several very close friends (BFFs), and she finds it necessary to share everything with them ("Well, I only told Roberta, the rumormonger, but she promised not to tell anyone"). Every day, she graces at least one of them with her presence at a two-hour lunch, and most evenings are spent dining out with friends. She also likes to be seen at "society events." Me, I'm just a poor old country boy (who fixes his own lunch), remember?

5. Her Communication Style: Details are essential. When she tells a story or answers a question, you get the l-o-n-g, unexpurgated version. In her mind, it's important to provide all the background and ancillary information, and the sundry details so she can be sure that you will "get it." Unfortunately, I am a Type A+ guy who seeks the bottom line, and quickly. Oil and water, so to speak. Kaboom! She gets pissed when I propose that she might condense her speech by suggesting "Short version, please." This raises Life Lesson 21.

Life Lesson 21: Never provide guidance to a queen.

Remember, she was born a guider, not a guidee.

6. Wine Snob: She has refined senses of taste and smell, and it reflects on her wine choices. She only drinks Pinot Noirs (when she is not sucking down Cosmopolitans). On the other hand, as a result of my PD, I lost my sense of smell, and I drink anything that is red except Pinot Noir which is too watery to me. If I can't chew it, I don't drink

it. The positive aspect to this is that she never drinks my wine. The negative side is that she likes expensive Pinot Noirs.

Queenly wine drinking also requires a built-in wine cooler to keep the (mostly) Pinots at the proper consumption temperature and multiple sets of wine glasses to choose from, depending on the occasion. Yep, we've got both. I should mention that I drink my chewy red wine from a Mason jar. (No, I don't make this stuff up.)

7. Shopaholic: She's a shopper, where I'm a buyer. I go to a store to buy something that I require (and get out of there pronto, Tonto). She goes to a store for the experience of shopping and maybe finding something that she "needs."

"Need" is her favorite verb. It is much more dramatic than "would like to have" or "would probably benefit from," and it conveys a sense of urgency. "Need" is an implicit royal decree.

Shopping to her is an event, like going to a movie or reading a book. Only once have I seen her swear off shopping.

One Saturday afternoon when visiting friends in Atlanta, the Queen and our friend Louise went shopping at the Lenox Square Mall in Buckhead. After two hours, they returned, way too early and scared shitless. While they were shopping, masses of people came running toward them yelling that shots had been fired! They searched for refuge and found a Prada store and went inside. Imagine that. There are 198 stores in the Lenox Mall. Did they go into a Chico's or Beall's or Best Buy??? No, it was Prada. Filled with luxury handbags, shoes and accessories. The store owner went from being disappointed that he was losing sales due to the situation to being ecstatic that he had the world's two best shoppers as a captive (literally) audience. Seriously, the store had an armed guard, and they escorted everyone into a back room. After 45 minutes, the police said, "All clear," and everyone could leave. It turns out that there wasn't a shooter or even a gun. It was a fight that broke out in the food court. Must have been bad sushi.

The good news is that the Queen vowed never to shop in a mall again. The bad news is (1) she forgot over time, and (2) Amazon.

She is Number 5 on Amazon Prime's Distinguished Buyers list. The Amazon delivery drivers know her by name; they call her Queenie. Every day seems like Christmas at our house when Amazon brings packages to the door. Old Saint Nick driving a smiley-arrow-logo truck. Ho! Ho! Ho!

8. Grocery Store Shopping: First of all, she must go to a grocery store daily, just like you brush your teeth, read a newspaper, etc. If she were to miss a day, there might be a hole on the sagging shelves of our refrigerator.

In a grocery store, my list is my Bible. (Thou shalt buy these, and only these, items!) Her list is merely an outline that is easily expanded as she sees items on the shelves.

She also believes that she needs to examine every package on the shelves for "leanness," the latest expiration date, caloric content, etc. She takes longer to select a steak than it takes me to grill it. – Me, I'm just happy that I found the section that the item is in, so I grab the nearest package of it and go.

9. Gourmet Cook: She is a chef – Me, I am a "shit hot" microwaver and griller. She prepares a meal to savor the experience – I cook because food is needed to keep me alive. She has around 150 cookbooks, of which 45 are by Ina Garten. Ina is her idol. When someone asks, "How did you make this?" she always starts with "Well, it's an Ina Garten recipe..." If I never heard the words "Ina Garten" again in my lifetime, I would be a happy camper. Fat, friggin chance of that happening.

10. Addictions: The Queen is addicted to TV. From the moment she rises (somewhere before noon) until bedtime (somewhere before 10 PM), she has the TV on. In the morning, it takes exactly five microseconds from when she enters the family room until the TV is tuned to one of the network pap espousers and giggles shows, e.g., *Good Morning America*, *Today*, etc. During the day, it is the Food Network channel (let's watch Guy Fieri eat another mega sandwich in another dive). When that's over, there's always Ina Garten (Ralph!). In the evening, it starts with the local news (what hurricane is bearing down on our sweltering island – excuse me, "key" – it's more upscale than "island" – or "cay," which adds a touch of *savoir faire* – "hotsy-totsy").

Then at exactly 6:30 PM EDT, the world comes to an end!!!!! David Muir comes on the *ABC World News Tonight* show and explains the impending Armageddon, e.g., "Category 10 hurricane headed for Florida. Market loses 10,000 points – largest single day loss ever. Democrats plan to impeach all Republicans, school boards and MBA's."

Makes you pee your pants and head for the good

old bomb shelter of the '50s. And after a half an hour of doom and gloom, he leaves us with "See you tomorrow evening." Life goes on.

As a footnote, I think Mark Twain expressed his thoughts on Armageddon quite well by commenting "If the world comes to an end, I want to be in Cincinnati. Everything comes there ten years later."

Then it's time for *Wheel of Fortune* and *Jeopardy*, where every viewer believes "I coulda been a contender!"

Finally, off to the bedroom to watch *Property Brothers* and *House Hunters* on HDTV or *Diners, Drive-Ins and Dives* and Ina on the Food Network channel. Life of the Xfinity junkie.

11. Promptness: Time is relative. Albert "Frizzy Al" Einstein said so. Unfortunately, I am a Type A+ guy who believes in punctuality. The Queen says that she does also; however, her definition of punctual is being in the neighborhood of the appointed hour. I figure that I spend an average of 20 minutes a day waiting for her. This means that over our 53 years together, I have waited about NINE MONTHS! I could have had a baby in that time. Well, maybe not. Every morning I must remind myself that patience is a virtue.

12. Requests: Any seemingly innocuous request is really a royal command. For example, if she says, "When you get a chance, could you please..." this is an order. It means drop what you are doing immediately and hop to it. Then report back to me when you're done. If you fail to act immediately, woe is you. Remember, just smile and say "Yes, dear."

13. Transportation: The preferred ride is a limo; however, everyone needs a personal vehicle for running errands. The Queen likes German convertibles, specifically the BMW 640i. Her Beemer is only used to go to the grocery store, hairdresser, CVS, doctor, gym, and car wash. She puts about 3,500 miles a year on it, but she always looks good getting there with the top down.

14. Her Appearance: Regarding her hair, blondes have more fun, and eventually all queens turn blonde. I think it happens at their coronations. And heaven forbid her ever exiting the palace without being fully camouflaged in makeup or not wearing the appropriately coordinated outfit that matches the day's planned activities. And she keeps up with pedicures and manicures: Pretty feet are happy feet, and every queen wants happy feet.

When we moved to Dallas, she gave up real estate and sold high-end clothes out of our house. She collected an amazing inventory of clothes, kinda like the demo models that the car salesman drives. Unfortunately, this hobby has continued into retirement. Our new house has six clothes closets – the four largest ones (walk-in closets) are "Queen only," one mini-closet is mine, and one is for guests. However, she uses the guest closet when no one is staying with us.

15. Her Travel Necessities: When we travel to and from our Pennsylvania fish camp, there is a minimum set of things she takes:

   a. Clothes equal to two times the duration of the

planned stay. She needs "choices," and she also must be able to adapt to variable weather;

b. Her pillow;

c. A portable makeup station;

d. Golf clubs, shoes, and clothes;

e. Wine bag;

f. Computer, iPad, iPhone;

g. Duplicates – Things that you can't buy in the other location or items that are needed to make sure the same things are available at both locations (it is an unwritten law that each royal household must be similarly equipped);

h. Wine for the Fish Camp – PA has government-run state stores with limited choices and high prices. BYOB!

i. Exercise outfits;

j. Dressy clothes (in case we are invited to a royal affair);

k. Gedunks – candy and goodies for the drive;

l. A cooler and sandwiches for the first day's lunch;

m. Nightlight for the motel room;

n. Prescriptions and vitamins for the stay;

o. Blanket to stay warm when she snoozes in the car.

This usually amounts to four suitcases, a golf bag, a clothes bag, a wine box, and many, many carry-on bags.

Me, I take golf clubs, a Dopp kit, a couple of Columbia fishing shirts, and several pairs of underwear.

Here come the Clampetts – our Audi Q7 SUV has 70 cubic feet of cargo space, and we use it all. Haven't had to tie Granny to the roof rack – yet!

I hope that you now have a better understanding of

a queen's needs and life behind the palace doors. Given this information, let's move on to Life Lessons about marriage.

Chapter 11: Marriage

Our long-lived marital union of 53 WONDERFUL years has taught me many valuable lessons that I feel compelled to share. Think of them as shortcuts to success – kinda like a Cliff Notes study guide to marriage.

The Institution

Groucho Marx once said, "Marriage is an institution, but who wants to live in an institution?" And Joey Adams, the actress, quipped, "Marriage is give and take. You'd better give it to her or she'll take it anyway." But enough quotage; let's get to real guidance that you can use.

There is an old adage that says, "True love is forever." Well, it's close to being correct, but Life Lesson 22 sets it straight.

Life Lesson 22: True love is not forever; eternity is. And some marriages seem to last an eternity.

[Note to Editor – I'm just kidding, dear. – End Note]

Remember this is only true for 50% of marriages. The other 50% end in divorce.

Divorce

Our 53 WONDERFUL years of marital bliss is a rarity today, when only 6% of all marriages last 50 years or more. In fact, this raises our next Life Lesson.

Life Lesson 23: Marriage is what you make it – most people make it a double.

Unfortunately, according to Banschick[vi] and Spector,[vii] the percent of marriages that end in divorce is 50%, and 80% of those divorcees remarry. Talk about a jinx – 67% of second marriages and 74% of third marriages fail. Herein lies Life Lesson 24.

Life Lesson 24: When it goes to shit, it goes to shit!

And these two lessons lead to Life Lesson 25.

Life Lesson 25: In marriage, if at first you don't succeed, quit while you still have half a house, half a car, and one set of alimony payments.

This reminds me of what a contractor who was painting the royal condo for us told me, "My two ex-wives were good housekeepers. Both of them kept the house when we got divorced."

But enough about divorce. Let's concentrate on what happens when you say "I do."

Dating vs. Marriage

Here is a test for the newlywed. Fill in your spouse's name in the first blank, add a number in the second blank, and then answer the multiple choice on duration:

I dated _____ for_____ (a. years, b. months, c. days, or d. hours).
Therefore, I know her well and what to expect in marriage.

WRONG-O, my naïve friend.
The playing field has changed. You're in the big leagues now, baby!

Remember your vow "what God has wrought" etc., etc., etc.? Partner, you are "wrought" now. Marriage is not easy-peasy. This brings us to Life Lesson 26.

Life Lesson 26: Opposites attract – then collide.

This is a derivative of Coulomb's Law. You remember crazy old Charlie Coulomb, don't you? (Actually, he was named Charles-Augustus de Coulomb. No wonder he went by "Crazy Charlie.")

Let me give you an example:

Albert "Frizzy Al" Einstein said, "Men marry women with the hope that they will never change. Women marry men with the hope that they will change. Invariably both will be disappointed."

Unfortunately, this causes Life Lesson 27.

Life Lesson 27: She snores, burps, and farts. Get over it!

Of course you never noticed this when you were dating. You were "in love," and you were blinded by this love. And a corollary to Life Lesson 27 is Life Lesson 28.

Life Lesson 28: Marriage has warts.

Advice to the Newlywed

[Note to Prospective Husbands – Have your wedding date tattooed somewhere on your body where she will never look (I'll leave it up to you to figure out where). That way, you can never forget it and suffer the "You don't love me; you don't even remember when we got married" whine. As an alternative strategy for those who fear the needle and ink or those who can't think of a "no see" location, get married on your birthday. That way, you won't forget. Consider this a freebie Life Lesson. No extra charge. – End Note]

The Secrets to A Successful Marriage.

You can win at this game. Remember you need to go along to get along.

First of all, words are emotional. One wrong word can ruin your next month. Therefore, I am going to give you two phrases that will calm the raging seas. This is Life Lesson 29.

Life Lesson 29: The correct answer to any question is:

"Yes, dear."

Or
"Whatever you say, sweetheart."

These two responses can be used interchangeably. OK, guys, you need to practice this. Every morning when you get up, I want you to do 50 repetitions of these two lines. Remember, the key is to look and sound believable. Practice in front of a mirror. You must look serious, and for Pete's sake, no smirking, grinning or winks! When you get proficient, try "Yes, sweetheart" or "Whatever you say, dear" to mix things up a bit.

I know you will thank me for this advice. I receive testimonials every day from guys writing how it saved their marriage.

One must also master the art of interpreting the unspoken word and the cryptic comment as captured in Life Lesson 30.

Life Lesson 30: No man is truly married until he understands every word his wife is NOT saying.

Here is a starter set of unspoken actions, ordered by

severity, and advice on what you should do and what you should NOT do:

1. She flips you the bird – Laugh it off and behind your back give her a double flip. You both will feel better.

2. She glares – Matador Warning – do not wave a red flag by glaring back. Then follow the advice in unspoken action #4 below.

3. She cries – Offer her a Kleenex, but don't suggest she should blow her nose. You can talk your way out of this, silver tongue.

4. She clams up, and you get the silent treatment – Do not attempt to talk to her. Stay out of sight and let it defuse. Create a DMZ (Demilitarized Zone). Talking is like breathing, and she can only hold her breath so long. When she opens up, be there with some "Yes, dears," "Whatever you say, sweethearts," and throw in a couple of "Mea culpas."

5. She throws your clothes out of the bedroom window onto the front lawn – Do not retaliate with her clothes (the amount of clothing would take you all day) or make some smart-ass comment like "Well, I guess that gives you more space for your stuff." My tactical advice is to get your valuables out of the house before she changes the locks on the doors.

6. She packs a bag and calls Uber – Do not (I

repeat, Do Not) ask her for a forwarding address or offer to drive her.

You may notice that I don't list any real DO actions for #5 and #6. That is because I am clueless. I have seen cases of both, and they all ended in divorce. If you experience either, you're on your own, Lone Ranger. Your life is about to become a country song.

There is also one unwritten rule that you must religiously practice that may piss you off, so to speak, but which is necessary for marital harmony. I implore you to follow Life Lesson 31.

Life Lesson 31: Put the toilet seat down when you are finished.

Look, I didn't make the rules, and it is just as easy for women to lift the seat as it is for guys to lower it. But they aren't concentrating when they squat, and you'll have hell to pay.

By the way, I'm lobbying for the Casual Friday Rule for Toilet Seats: on Fridays we leave the seat vertical. If you want to support this movement, tweet me at @PottyParity.

And of course, there is no substitute for silence. Life Lesson 32, which is credited to Albert "Frizzy Al" Einstein, says:

Life Lesson 32: If you are wrong and shut up, you are a wise man. If you're right and you shut up, you are married.

Hey, I'm beginning to like this guy, Frizzy Al. I might even add him to the list of my favorite humor writers. **[Note to Dave Barry – Don't worry, Dave, you're still Numero Uno on the list. – End Note]**

Polygamy

I believe most men will agree that monogamy (having one wife at a time) is at a minimum more than sufficient, perhaps bordering on excessive. However, some religions have practiced polygamy over time. Brigham Young, one-time leader of the Mormon Church, is quoted by Mark Twain as saying, "Take my word for it, ten or eleven wives is all you need—never go over it." I don't know about you, but this thought sends cold chills up and down my spine. Given my luck, I'd end up with a palace full of queens. Can I get an amen here?

How The Queen And I Have Stayed Together

You might ask how our marriage has lasted. We have had our share of problems and battles. The secret is two threats which she made early in our relationship:

1. If you cheat on me, I will super-glue one part of

your body to your belly – a modern-day Lorna Bobbitt; and

2. You can't afford a divorce.

Simple, but effective.

And so, I move on to Lessons Learned during my career, with this parting thought as Life Lesson 33.

Life Lesson 33: When you have a Queen, don't reshuffle the deck and end up with a Joker.

Chapter 12:
Career Lessons

I've already provided an overview of my career, and I won't bore you with the details of the 42 years; however, I have learned a number of lessons that I can share, and I will include additional memoir information to illustrate these Life Lessons.

Let's start with Life Lesson 34, which is foundational.

Life Lesson 34: You must decide early on if you want a job or a career.

A job is what you have to do to bring home the bacon. A career is what you want to do and where you want to go. A good illustration of this is what happened to me when I went to sign up for Medicare. The agent, Mister John Doe (they don't give their real names, and I guess that's understandable), looked at my earnings history and said, "You must have worked real (sic) hard during your career." I answered, "Yes, I guess I did." He said, "I couldn't do that. That's why I have this government job."

He was right. He had a job.

A career is an occupation for a significant period of time which offers opportunities for advancement.

A job is comfortable; a career is challenging and dolorous. Dolorous – now there is another word that is worth the price of this book alone. Say it out loud, you thesaurusite, you. It means harrowing or painful.

As I said, you have to decide where you want to go with your career. As Yogi Berra noted, "If you don't know where you are going, you might wind up someplace else."

Opportunity

To set the stage, my definition of "opportunity" is a chance to learn something new or to do something new.

The most-quoted idiom about opportunity is – Opportunity knocks but once. Close, but no cigar, Groucho. Life Lesson 35, which is consistent with Oprah Winfrey's comments on opportunity, corrects this saying.

Life Lesson 35: Opportunity doesn't knock; it whispers. You must always be listening for it.

So picture this – you've got your nose to the grindstone, ear to the ground, feet planted firmly, etc., etc., etc. (Yada! Yada! Yada! in Seinfeld-speak), and hark, you think you hear Opportunity whisper. What to do, Mister Contortionist?

Don't fear, laddie. The answer is Life Lesson 36.

Life Lesson 36: Never say no to an opportunity.

When I was asked to move to Maryland and take over our facility in the DC area, and when I was given a chance to move to Texas to lead a large division of E-Systems, many of my State College colleagues said, "How could you leave Happy Valley and give up this utopia?" To them, stability was important. But I looked at each of these two opportunities as a chance to gain new experiences. And I was right.

As Davy Crockett said when leaving Tennessee for the Alamo, "You can all go to Hell, and I'm going to Texas." Well, of course, I was more subtle than that in my departure.

Another point to be made is if you're going to play the game, play to win. Life Lesson 37 is succinct.

Life Lesson 37: Don't half-ass anything. Always use your full ass.

Of course, the corollary to this is Life Lesson 38.

Life Lesson 38: Each day, do more than is expected of you, and before long, more will be expected of you.

The half-empty-glass guy sees this as additional work. The half-full-glass guy sees this as opportunity for promotion.

Who's Your Daddy?

During the 42 years of my career, I really only worked for one company, which is a rarity today, but I survived five acquisitions (four from the acquiree's side, one with the acquirer). One could look at this as a loss – when an acquisition occurs, you lose the credentials that you have worked to establish and are thrown into an uncomfortable "prove yourself again" situation. But that is the half-empty-glass perspective once more. It's showtime, baby! Cowboy up and make it happen. Life Lesson 39 is a common theme in management literature.

Life Lesson 39: Change creates opportunity.

My career development occurred in a dynamic, evolving organization due to acquisitions, mergers, and reorganizations. Calling it dynamic and evolving is like saying the Summer Olympics is a track meet, or King Kong is a monkey, or politicians earn a "comfortable living" (40% of Congress are millionaires). Let me recap the fluidness that was going on.

In 1948, three moonlighting physics professors at Penn State (Haller, Raymond, and Brown) founded HRB to build intelligence surveillance equipment and systems for the US government and military, and in 1958, Singer, the sewing machine company, purchased HRB, which became HRB Singer. Did you know that treadle on the sewing machine was actually an antenna for intercepting signals? (Hey – pulling your chain, but it could have been.)

I started at HRB Singer in 1966.

In 1988, the Singer CEO died suddenly, and in the uncertainty that followed, Singer was acquired by a corporate raider, a real-life Gordon Gecko from the movie *Wall Street*, who believed he could sell the thirteen business units separately for more than he paid for them as a company. However, his message to all was "I'm here to do what's best for the country and the employees." (Benevolent and patriotic-sounding guy, right?) HRB Singer became HRB Systems. After a public auction that went on for months, he sold the thirteen units for more than he paid for Singer, and he did what was best – but that was what was best for "Gordon Gecko." (Surprise! Surprise! Surprise!) Hence, Life Lesson 40.

Life Lesson 40: Beware of a man saying he wants to do the right thing – it usually means the right thing for *him*.

The usual grouping of "right-thing-ers" includes corporate raiders, politicians, televangelists, etc.

To quote Willie "the Pen" Shakespeare, "Alas, poor 'Yorick' Gecko." He was sentenced to four years in prison for securities and tax fraud on another of his acquisitions. Funny, I don't recall any "Free Gordon" write-in campaigns by ex-Singer employees. I wonder why?

HRB Systems was sold to Hadson, an oil and natural gas company out of Oklahoma City (a group of free-wheeling wildcatters who couldn't spell "defense"). The only thing they knew was that they had previously acquired a small "space" company as an incidental piece of an electric utility acquisition, and they decided to double down on defense. And yes, Alex Trebek, they made it a true "daily double." They paid twice what we were worth! HRB became HRB Systems, a Hadson Company.

In 1990, the energy sector went to hell, and Hadson couldn't service their debt, so we were sold to E-Systems, a large, established defense and intelligence firm out of Dallas (for a price that Hadson should have paid), a move that rekindled our growth. We became HRB Systems, an E-Systems Division. I moved to Texas in 1994 to become General Manager of the E-Systems Garland Division.

And the defense industry consolidation continued. In 1995, Raytheon bought E-Systems, and in 1997 acquired the defense electronics business of Texas Instruments and Hughes. I became the VP, Imagery and Geospatial Systems Division, which contained business units from legacy E-Systems, TI and Hughes. In 2002, Raytheon reorganized, creating six businesses, and I became a Raytheon VP and President, Raytheon Intelligence and Information Systems.

And the consolidation still continues. Raytheon and United Technologies just completed a merger in 2020.

Life Lesson 41: Size matters (in the defense business).

During the mid-1990's the Department of Defense encouraged industry consolidation to control costs and promote efficiency, and in the early 2000s, the Secretary of Defense, Donald Rumsfeld, defined a major top-to-bottom reorganization of the DoD to meet future needs and to address DoD efficiencies. I'm not sure either really worked as planned.

By the way, I met Donald Rumsfeld at a White House event in 2004. I was introduced as a Raytheon exec with E-Systems heritage, and he recalled several prior E-Systems leaders he knew. I said something like "Well, you're probably right, I only joined E-Systems nine years ago," and he let loose with that staccato machine-gun speech that we have all heard on TV: "Of course I'm right. I said it, didn't I?" Then he laughed like hell, and we all relaxed.

Teamwork

Almost all of today's business projects are large and complex enough to require a team of various skills to complete. One day a senior system engineer was briefing me on a project, and he repeatedly used the word "I," e.g., I did this, and I did that. In my role as a coach, I said to him, "Remember, there is no 'I' in team," to which he responded, "No, but there is one in 'Kiss my ass.'" And so ended the lesson for the day!

Bragging and Braggarts

Everyone wants to position themselves positively; however, it should be done with actions and results, not with words. Contrary to their objective of telling the world about their achievements, braggarts are really addressing their shortcomings, i.e., nobody knows about them.

> **Life Lesson 42: If someone has to brag about his "success," it means that others don't recognize it.**

I can also state it simpler in Life Lesson 43.

> **Life Lesson 43: Bragging and farting have a lot in common: they both**

make a lot of noise and often stink. The difference is that the braggart wants to be recognized, and the farter does not.

Business meetings

Meetings are a necessary evil. It is important to get the group's ideas and have everyone on the same page, but remember Life Lesson 44, which is a spinoff of a Dave Barry quote:

Life Lesson 44: Work would be productive if meetings didn't get in the way.

To avoid a meeting "time quagmire," you must exercise control, or "It's déjà vu all over again," as Yogi Berra would say.

Unfortunately, in meetings, some people act as if they're being paid by the word. They revel in their eloquence. These are usually the ones that don't have anything to say. Even Plato recognized this way back in the BC days when he said, "Wise men speak because they have something to say; fools because they have to say something."

To avoid this "blathering," consider Life Lesson 45, which is a Gaelic proverb about thinking before you speak.

Life Lesson 45: Be sure to taste your words before you spit them out.

I have also developed a rule for business meetings in Life Lesson 46.

Life Lesson 46: To have a productive meeting you must adhere to the Go and Stop principles.

By this I mean start the meeting on time (Go) and limit the discussion to one hour (Stop). If you can't decide on something in one hour, you won't get there.

I think it is also important in business to respect your colleagues by being on time. I had a CEO once who said, "Early is on time." In business and in life, promptness matters.

I also had a CEO who reminded me, "We're not in this for a religious experience, we're in business." But that's another story.

Be Decisive

To lead, one must consider the options, make a decision, communicate it clearly, and act. The wishy-washies ain't gonna do it. Life Lesson 47 captures this.

Life Lesson 47: Be decisive. Right or wrong, make a decision. The road of life is paved with flat squirrels who couldn't make a decision.

The Customer

If the customer is always right, your job is to translate his "rightiness" into the realm of possible actions.

Remember – without a customer, a business does not exist.

Friends often ask me what I miss about work. I tell them three things:

1. I miss the people I worked with. This was my extended family.

2. I miss the projects that we did. We did some cool shit.

3. I miss our customers. We worked with some of the greatest people in the government and in industry.

I don't miss the rest of the things that went along with the position.

If It Doesn't Work Out

What happens if you fail? There is a Life Lesson that covers you.

Life Lesson 48: If at first you don't succeed, there's always the Marketing Department.

Just screwing with you. Of course, the answer is to learn from it and try, try again. Most times you will learn more from mistakes than from successes.

I will end this chapter with the fear that I am beginning to sound like a guidance counselor or Joel Osteen, the mega-church televangelist who preaches positive attitude.

Permit me one final story on how positive employees are essential to business and one Dave Barry quote.

I was in Mike's Restaurant in Annapolis, Maryland, the local crab house. The waitress, a Baltimorean straight out of *Hairspray*, with a bleached head of hair gathered in a tight beehive, was taking our orders, and I said I'd like to have calamari. She said to me, "Do you know what that is, hon?" (Everyone in the Baltimore area is addressed as "hon.") I said, "Yes." She said, "It's squid." I said, "Yes." She said, "Have you ever had it before?" I said, "Yes." (You can begin to see from this dialogue what a suave conversationalist I am.) She incredulously said, "And you're going to have it again?"

What's the message? It's a good thing that Mike's sells crabs because they're sure as hell not selling calamari. In addition, I doubt that my waitress ever became Mike's restaurant manager.

Now, WDDBS, What Did Dave Barry Say about his chosen career as an author?

"Don't you wish you had a job like mine? All you have to do is think up a certain number of words! Plus, you can repeat words! And they don't even have to be true!"

While we are discussing careers and words, let me address a pet peeve –– ManagementSpeak. In the course of business (and also life), we repeatedly run into words that are overused or meaningless and that grate on us. We need to strike them from the English language. Let me give you my list.

Chapter 13:
ManagementSpeak
– Kill These Words

ManagementSpeak is a language used in conference rooms and on PowerPoint slides around the world. It is a trendy set of impressive-sounding words that make something appear more important or profound than it actually is. It is apparently taught in business schools and military Officer Candidate Schools since the graduates of this training speak it proficiently.

I probably sound like the cranky old man sitting on a park bench mumbling, but after 42 years in business, I have a list of these words that make me cringe when I hear them. If I had my way, I would make using these words a misdemeanor. Since I can't do that, I have initiated a campaign to discourage their use. If you care to join me, the next time you are in a meeting and someone repeatedly uses these words, raise a yellow penalty card, like a soccer referee does to indicate a foul. You will either be escorted out of the meeting or the speaker will think twice before using that word again. As a note of caution, don't do this if the speaker is higher up on the organization chart than you (just bite your tongue and smile).

Here is my Irritation List:

1. Synergy – a made-up word to justify acquisitions and mergers. The theory is that by combining two organizations, we can cut costs and be more productive. Remember I said it is made-up. It really is a euphemism for layoffs.

2. Share – a word used extensively in nonprofit organizations. It's a feel-good word, used like this: "Let me share this experience with you." I've been in meetings where one presenter "shared" fifteen things in ten minutes. I felt warm and fuzzy enough to break into a chorus of Kumbaya!

3. Garner – as in "we will garner the benefits of our efforts." What the hell? Is this taught in Management 101?

4. Strategy – a strategy is just a plan with Power-Point slides.

5. Integrate – the past pluperfect tense of ingrate, an ungrateful person.

6. Symbiotic – a mutually beneficial relationship between different people or groups. Symbiotic alliances are how you purportedly achieve synergy (magic fairy dust).

7. Proactive – an action word that once meant "gung-ho" but is now a wimpy "be prepared."

8. Scenario – a business scenario is a view of a possible future environment based on assumptions about uncertainties which face a business, i.e.,

"Maybe this. Maybe that." Therefore, we need to develop a strategy to symbiotically garner synergy in our scenarios. I just scored a five-pointer in ManagementSpeak.

9. Thinking techniques (Think outside the box, Blue Sky thinking, Brainstorming) – techniques that mean "I'm stumped – got any wild-ass ideas?"

10. Core competency – a concept in management theory which means "a harmonized combination of multiple resources and skills that distinguish a firm in the marketplace" and is the foundation of a company's competitiveness. The simple translation is "what we do best that the other guys can't match."

11. TechnoSpeak – And what about TechnoSpeak, which is a branch of ManagementSpeak? It is the language of the hot, hot, hot startups and technology giants of today. Gary Trudeau recently captured the following TechnoSpeak in one Sunday Doonesbury strip:
    a. All hands meeting
    b. Passion for engagement
    c. Leveraging the future
    d. Light-bulb moment
    e. Reached out
    f. Circled back
    g. World-changing vision
    h. Team-centric paradigm
    i. Revolutionizing
    j. Our vision

k. You are the disruptors

My advice to the aspiring young techies out there in Bookland – memorize this list, and when you are giving a presentation, throw a few random terms into your pitch. It will make you a "Rockstar."

While we are discussing ManagementSpeak, what about other annoying, overused words that we see and hear every day? I have a few that I could live without:

12. Brexit – the press's most overused word of 2019. The Brits and the European Union pissed around with this until the whole world was screaming "Get-Er-Done," in the words of Larry the Cable Guy.

13. New and Improved – this is adspeak. Who wouldn't want "new and improved"? The other choice is "old and stagnant." Not me, pardner, I want that titillating new shit. Unfortunately, "new and improved" usually means the product is smaller and it costs more.

14. MSRP (Manufacturer's Suggested Retail Price) – This is a fictitious dollar amount that appears on new cars' window stickers. It has no meaning. If you buy a car for the MSRP, then I have a bridge in Brooklyn that you might be interested in. This is not the only fictitious number on the sticker – there's also the estimated gas mileage. Hah, and double Hah!

15. Middle Class – the imaginary group that about

90% of Americans think they belong to. Therefore, every politician makes stump speeches about
their support for this group.

16. Tax Neutral – this oxymoron is like "perpetual
    motion." It sounds good, but it ain't gonna hap-
    pen.

17. Farm to Table – this is a phrase used by restau-
    rants to justify menu price increases.

18. Cost of Living – the level of prices relating to a
    range of everyday items which was invented by
    economists and is understood only by economists
    and Harvey Smidlapp of Boise, Idaho.

19. Hi Def – a catch-all phrase to describe any prod-
    uct made after the year 2000. No one would be
    caught dead today with a Low Def item.

Speaking of words that need to be killed, let's "segue"
to Retirement and Geezerville.

Chapter 14:
Retirement and Geezerville

I retired from Raytheon in February 2009. The Queen was worried at that time about what I would do in retirement since I was the guy that did everything "FULL ASS" at work for 42 years.

I have to tell you it was a smooth transition. I initially did some consulting, and I served out my second term on the NOAA Science Advisory Board. I also chaired a NOAA review on Climate and Satellites.

Upon retirement, we relocated to Geezerville. This is my pet name for the Sarasota, Florida area, home to retirees, senior citizens, snowbirds, and curmudgeons of all flavors. Canadian geese also hang out here and crap on our lawns (hey, I said Canadian geese, not Canadians – touchy folks, those hosers, as Wayne and Garth would say, eh?)

This chapter focuses on the demographics of Geezerville and retirement activities.

Demographics

Prior to my retirement, we purchased a condo on Lido Key, a barrier island off Sarasota, Florida. A barrier island is a long, narrow island lying parallel and close to the mainland, protecting the mainland from erosion and storms. You might know it by its meteorological name:

"hurricane magnet." It serves the same function for tropical storms as a trailer park does for tornadoes. Sarasota has eight barrier islands including Bird Key, Siesta Key, Lido Key, Casey Key, and Longboat Key. All are at an elevation of three feet. No nosebleeds here, but you'd better be able to float!

Sarasota, on the southwest coast of Florida, is situated between Tampa Bay and Naples. According to the Chamber of Commerce, it is known for its cultural amenities including the Sarasota Opera, the Sarasota Orchestra, the Asolo Repertory Theater, Van Wezel Performing Arts Hall, the John and Mable Ringling Museum of Art, the Chalk Festival (artists drawing amazing three-dimensional paintings on the streets in chalk), and Thunder By The Bay (an annual Harley get-together every January to enjoy "hell-raising" culture). As a result of all these resources, I am able to keep my Culture-O-Meter pegged. The culture tank overfloweth.

Sarasota is also known for its fine white-sand beaches, resorts, and medical facilities.

The fine white sand is both a blessing and a curse. The local beaches have been consistently rated as among the best in the world, and Siesta Key was #1 in 2015 according to "Dr. Beach," who is the world-recognized "sand guru." (I am not making any of this up; in fact, I wish that I were. I mean "Dr. Beach" and "sand guru"? –– Give me a break.) But Mother Nature is Mother Nature, and currents and storms cause beach erosion over time, creating the need for replenishment. This is costly and creates family friction between the sister islands, who worry that dredging sand from another island's pass will cause erosion of their sand. This causes discontent, lawsuits, protests, and delays. Life is not always a bed of roses here in Paradise.

The Sarasota area is believed to have been discovered by Spanish explorers when Hernando de Soto came to Florida. Hernando "The Wuss" soon tired of the heat, humidity, and killer pythons, and moved to Detroit where he started the DeSoto car company which made Chrysler DeSotos until 1960.

Sarasota has become a mecca for retirees and snow-birds.

I refer to the Sarasota area as Geezerville. Some people call it God's Waiting Room or Senior City or Walker-town. It is filled with old people.

To illustrate, the median age in the United States is 37. The median age in Sarasota is 45. But the median age on Longboat Key is 71.2! WHOO-EEE, turn out the lights – the party's over! Life in the fast lane with a cane![viii]

You can contrast this with The Villages, a retirement community in Sumter County, Florida with a population of 123,000 people and a median age of 70.6 – wee tod-dlers.[ix]

By the way, The Villages is perhaps best known for its golf courses: 12 championship courses and 38 nine-hole executive courses, and for its sexually transmitted disease (STD) statistics that were reported by several newspapers a couple of years ago. Apparently, this STD "surge" was exaggerated, but many today still believe that the town puts Viagra in the water. **[Note to Self – Contact the Longboat Key town council about this potential enhance-ment to the island. – End Note]**

For the first ten years of retirement, we lived in our condo on Lido Key. In February 2019, we moved into a house on Longboat Key. OK, readers, this is a test – What's wrong with this picture?

You got it right. The accepted norm is that as people age, they're supposed to downsize and move into condos and apartments where everything is taken care of. We forgot to read the literature. No lemmings here. Just call us trailblazers. Wait, make that "old trailblazers."

Longboat Key is the largest of Sarasota's barrier islands. It is split between two counties, Sarasota and Manatee. Legend says that Longboat Key got its name from the longboats left by the Spanish explorers once they reached land (their fearless leader "Chicken Juan" Anasco believed the natives were hostile and ordered his troops to flee). It was separated from Sarasota city in 1920 as a result of John "Mr. Circus" Ringling's lobbying to avoid taxes on his planned development of the island. The conventional wisdom is that "it's not what you know, it's who you know." In this case, that was probably extended to Life Lesson 49.

Life Lesson 49: It's not who you know – it's who you can buy.

Longboat Key has a year-round population of 7,000 people, but in the "season" (December through Easter, when the Northeast and Midwest aren't fit for human habitation), the snowbirds swell it to 24,000. Can you say "traffic jams in my neighborhood, Mr. Rogers"? Everyone just shrugs their shoulders, says, "Well, it's the season," and considers moving to the mainland.

However, the Sarasota city fathers are doing everything they can to discourage migration. For example, in the middle of this influx, they are closing down lanes of travel in order to construct multiple traffic circles on Route 41 in the city. If you have a traffic snarl, closing down lanes will make the situation snarlier, both in terms of congestion and the drivers' state of mind.

And do you astute readers see any inconsistencies here? Let's mix old drivers and multi-lane traffic circles and see what we get – dynamite! Remember Sarasota is a place where parking meters were installed, then removed because they were too high-tech for the residents to use. Now it's multi-lane traffic circles?

But let's get back to the demographics of Old Geezerville, Longboat Key.

Needless to say, there are few if any children on the island. In fact, I watch the local school bus drive up and down our main street, Gulf of Mexico Drive, every day looking for kids to pick up. But they don't exist.

Driving in Florida

If you want to do something fun on a sunny afternoon, go to Sarasota and watch the old people drive.

First of all, if you're in a car following them, they look like Q-tips: all you can see is a white cotton puff on the headrest.

The next thing to look for, a sure sign of a snowbird driver, is a collection of baseball caps in the back window of a Buick sedan.

And look for the oversized wrap-around Solar Shield sunglasses, the kind that resemble large, colored safety goggles.

I should also mention that turn signals are optional: maybe yes, maybe no.

And of course turns can be made from any lane: left turns from the right lane, right turns from the left lane, and all combinations thereof.

No one ever drives the speed limit here. You're either crawling along at a snail's pace or you're going like a bat out of hell.

As a result of all this quirky driving, the first thing I did when I got to Florida was sell my motorcycle. I want lots of iron around me in this environment, which often resembles a street version of the carnival ride Bumper Cars.

And here's a final reminder to senior drivers – on multi-lane highways, particularly Interstates, the left-hand lane is dedicated to seniors. Get out there and stay out there. It belongs to you. You earned it!

Other Senior Activities

Another place to watch old people is in supermarkets. Be careful, though, or they'll run you over with their carts or their electric scooters. And they either flunked or forgot math (just look at the number of items in their carts at the "10 Items or Less" checkout counters). It's also note-worthy that they can't find their cars when they go out, and they walk around, all over the parking lot, pushing their remote buttons and waiting for a beep.

As a side note, I studied supermarket purchases on Longboat Key, and the big volume items are from the pharmacy, the alcohol section, and Depends.

And I can't leave out dining, especially the Early Bird

Specials. If you ain't there about four, you ain't there. The number-one sport in Sarasota is dining out. Apparently no one cooks. Watch how they dress up for "supper" – shorts and shirt combinations of plaids and stripes, black socks in tennis shoes, and the *coup de grace* (French for killer touch), a white belt. All decked out for a night, or more accurately an afternoon, on the town. Fire up the Buick, Martha. We're going out to Red Lobster. We are going to paint the town beige! (Painting the town red is out of the question.)

One thing I never expected in Geezerville was that a significant Amish community resides here. They have a section of the city called Pinecraft. Apparently, the Amish elders leave their kids in charge of the farms for the northern winters and take buses to Sarasota for the season. I assume that they leave their horses and buggies back home in Ohio because you see them on their three-wheel bikes, wearing their traditional garb and flip-flops, heading to the beach to fish. Their rules are apparently looser in the south, and I guess whatever happens in Sarasota, stays in Sarasota.

Retiree Life Highlights

There are certain highlights to a retiree's life.

For example, filling your pill reminder box for the week. In fact, I looked at my calendar for the last year, and I found that the majority of my events included doctors' appointments, medical tests, dining out, and travel. La vida loca (wild and crazy times)!

Another favorite retiree activity is spending an afternoon at Costco. First of all, we start off with the retiree's lunch, a foot-long hot dog with sauerkraut and unlimited refills of soda for $1.59. Is this a great country or what? Then it's off to the wine area of the megastore. By volume, Costco is the number-one wine seller in the United States. They are also the number-one seller of toilet paper. (Coincidence? I think not.) Then as you shop, there are the grazing stations where food samples are divvied out to the lines of people who are apparently starving, but you wouldn't know it to look at their body shapes. After we load up on bulk amounts of toilet paper, water, wine, beer, vitamins, etc., we check out and head back to the island. We have charged $500 to our Costco credit card, but we have enough provisions to weather the next hurricane. Another exhausting day in the life of a retiree.

By the way, when you are retired, people invariably ask you what you did before retirement. If it's someone you would rather avoid, say "I married into money." That usually shuts them up.

Chapter 15:
Condo Life

As I mentioned, when we came to Sarasota in 2009, we moved into a relatively new condo. That's condo as in condominium, not "condom-is-numb," for all of you who just gasped when you read the sentence. Get your mind out of the gutter. Have you been drinking the water from The Villages?

Condo life is unique – you give up a lot of your privacy for the convenience of being able to walk away and have somebody else take care of things.

Our condo was two high-end, high-rise buildings with 54 units, located on the beach at Lido Beach. For reference, a high-rise building on Lido is eleven stories. We were on the seventh floor with great views of the Gulf, Sarasota Bay, and the city.

Here's one for you – "Lido" means beach in Italian. So I guess we lived on Beach Beach? Even we seniors can't forget that.

The condo had all the amenities and conveniences. In addition to our unit, we had a gym, social room and bar, dining room, catering kitchen, game room, library, and guest suites available for situations where you might have an overflow of guests or you didn't want them staying with you, e.g., mother-in-law, crying grandbabies, etc. We also had a pool, spa, outside party area, and a beach on the Gulf. And we were protected by 24/7 guard service. We had a general manager, concierges, mainte-nance staff, and cleaning personnel.

But we had never lived in a condo before. We had some adjustments to make.

Noise was rarely an issue. The condos were well con-structed and quiet. However, every time you went out-side your unit, there were people. Get on the elevator – people. Get the mail – people. Use one of the common facilities – people. Privacy went down the old too-too.

Only a small portion of our owners were year-round residents. The majority were part-timers. And unfor-tunately, the part-timers often treated the place like a hotel, not a home. If you are a Type A+ person (*a la moi*, for my French readers), it was annoying to see this devil-may-care attitude, particularly given the king's ransom we paid for our unit.

The worst violators were the guests of owners who were not in residence. They had no clue as to the rules and consequently ran amok.

But I am starting to sound like your crotchety, old codger neighbor who yells at the kids to stay off his lawn. I'll have another sip of wine and things will be better.

Of course, condo life, like everything else, is governed by the universal 5/95 Rule for Population Segregation. (For more about the 5/95 Rule, see Chapter 26.) How-ever, the specific 5/95 Rule in this case is: 5% of the own-ers are assholes, and that 5% take up 95% of the staff's time.

For example, we had residents who never put the facilities back after using them, e.g., hoses used to wash cars, gym equipment, etc. They believed that was the job of the concierge and maintenance staff.

We also had owners who went around leaving trash as a "test" to see if the staff was doing their job in keeping the facility clean. And there were whiners – constantly complaining about perceived issues.

But 95% of the residents were great people, and we made some good friends there. The majority of the owners were very successful businesspeople, either still working or retired. They had high expectations about their environment, including the condo. And they demanded the best. (P.S. The Queen was in her element at the eleven-story palace.)

To illustrate what a masochist, doofus, and do-gooder I am, I was on the condo board of directors for eight years, and I served as president of the board for five of those years. Are you laughing your asses off out there in Readerland? Well, I'm not making this up. I did it because I thought I could help run the enterprise. The worst parts of the position were dealing with the 5-percenters and conducting the board meetings. The 5-percenters were relentless in pursuing their causes. They never took NO for an answer. As Yogi said, "It was déjà vu all over again," and again, and again...

And the board meetings dragged on and on due to the 5-percenters repeating their arguments ad infinitum, which is Latin for "Is it dark yet?" These people thought Robert's Rules of Order was a foreign language.

Otherwise, I did enjoy my time on the board, and I am pleased with the results we collectively achieved.

One final story about condo life. The elevator is your conduit to the outside world.

How long is one and a half hours? It is 90 minutes, 5,400 seconds, 5,400,000 milliseconds, 5,400,000,000 microseconds. No, it's a friggin eternity when you are stuck alone in an elevator! One football Saturday I was watching the Penn State game on TV, and at half time, I got on the elevator to go for the mail. Bad move! About six inches down, no go – everything stopped. An hour and half later, the technician from Otis arrived and saved me. Good news – I was recording the game so I didn't miss anything – I had visited the restroom before I got on the elevator – and PSU won. Just another fun night in Geezerville. This leads to an important Life Lesson.

Life Lesson 50: Never go anywhere without first stopping by the LOO.

This becomes a critical, MUST-DO rule as one ages. Remember, "prostate" is a medical term for "poor state" of the enlarged gland!

The "Fish Camp"

This started out so simple. After our house in Dallas sold, I decided it would be nice to buy a fish camp where I could commune with nature and do some fly fishing for trout. Unfortunately, the way it has turned out is kinda like Eddie Albert and Eva Gabor on *Green Acres*. Little did I know how the Queen could "out-Eva" Eva! My dream was a private, cabin-type structure on a stream in the woods of Pennsylvania. However, cabin and Queen aren't compatible. Silly me. What was I thinking? A fish camp to her meant a structure that meets Queenly standards with proximity to restaurants, hairdressers, grocery stores, and her friends. So, after a series of "Yes, dear" and "Whatever you say, sweetheart" platitudes, we compromised and purchased a townhouse in historic Boalsburg, PA, deep in the heart of Happy Valley. The premise was that I (we) can spend April fishing in PA and then come back up when hurricane season attacks Florida.

Next, we had to buy another car so that we could leave one in PA and have the flexibility of flying in and out. But we couldn't buy a used one (my original naïve, foolish plan) because "you never know who might have owned it."

This is best summed up as a Life Lesson.

Life Lesson 51: Marriage takes the simple out of the equation.

We became a bi-HOA-community couple, with a condo in Sarasota, FL and a townhouse in Boalsburg, PA. Since the fish camp was in a 55-and-older community, we continued to live among our peers, the geezers.

The Decision to Move from Our Condo to a House

Given our age and our health issues, why did we want to swim upstream like mating salmon?

Let me summarize the factors in the decision.

1. We wanted more privacy. I don't want to be restricted by condo documents and bylaws. If I feel like cranking up the sound system and rockin' to the Rolling Stones, I'll do it.

2. The Queen is a gourmet cook, and the condo kitchen was adequate at best. The new kitchen is three times the size of the condo unit's kitchen.

3. I wanted an enclosed garage and a workbench and tools. In the condo, I had two parking spaces in a first-floor "parking lot." Now I have a two-car garage with TWO workbenches in it.

4. We were in the condo for ten years, and the appliances, air conditioning, etc. were reaching their end of life. We had already replaced several appliances. The house is newly built, and we should have another ten years before replacement becomes an issue.

5. We are 74 years old. If we wait to move, we will never do it.

So now you can see our logic, and as before, it rates a "partial truthiness" if you measure me by the newspapers' Politifact Test (fact-check test) – "Is John Doe Telling the Truth When He Says...?"

The real driver was that we fell in love with the new house.

As a footnote, the Queen was on a royal redo of the condo prior to all of this happening. She had the laundry room redone with washer/dryer/cabinet replacement and a wine cooler added, new backsplashes on all countertops, new dishwasher, all lighting replaced with LEDs, etc. Our timing sucked like a Hoover vacuum cleaner. Oh well, *c'est la vie* (roughly translated as "tough tooties").

Chapter 16:
Neighbors and Friends

They always say "friends and neighbors," but remember, in the Author's Introduction, there is a Life Lesson that says one should challenge what "They say." So I am going to do so and start with neighbors. Take that, you traditionalists!

The subject of neighbors is extremely complex from a biblical perspective. The Bible tells us, "Love thy neighbor." However, the Tenth Commandment says, "Thou shall not covet thy neighbor's wife or his ass." So how do we reconcile this conundrum (another $10 word worth the price of this book)?

This love/covet "neighbor stuff" is a potentially thorny topic, and before we begin to sound like a steamy paperback novel, I'm returning to Memoirland. If you are curious and want to explore it, I suggest reading Dr. Ruth or Dr. Phil or Jerry Springer (who, by the way, resides on Bird Key, Sarasota, USA). We got it all here in Geezerville, folks.

While I am digressing (only critics would call it rambling), did you know that when the circus was headquartered in Sarasota, the Ringling Brothers and Barnum & Bailey Circus ran a clown college that trained 1,400 clowns from 1968 until 1997? Some of the graduates went into the circus, but most became politicians. Whoa, enough meandering. Let's get back to neighbors.

I mentioned that after living in a trailer, free-loading in a fraternity house, and renting several apartments, the Queen-To-Be and I scraped together enough money for a down payment on our first house and began living the life of June and Ward Cleaver. Our first house was one of three new bilevels on a cul-de-sac (literally a high-class word for dead end) called Abbey Place. **[Note to Stephen King – You may want to consider "Cul-De-Sac" as a future novel title and topic. It has a double entendre kinda thingie. From your fellow author and Geezerville resident. – End Note]**

Little did we know about who would become our neighbors in the other two houses or in the house behind two of cul-de-sac lots!

Let me describe the 'hood. Again, the names have been changed to protect my butt.

Dr. Turf – The Watson Family

When we moved into our house, the lawn was in terrible shape. It had the contractor's mix of grass and weeds, or more accurately weeds and grass. I worked hard with Scott's Weed and Feed to get it in shape, and I was proud of the results. You could see the property line between my green lawn and the brown lawn next door.

Several months later, the Watsons moved in. One day, I looked out the front window and couldn't believe my eyes. I cried out to the Queen: "You've got to see this. You won't believe what this asshole is doing." My new neighbor was rototilling up all his grass. He then reseeded it and soon after started mowing it with a golf course blade-type greens' mower. Within weeks his lawn looked like a putting green, and you could see our lot line again, this time highlighted by his emerald grass.

It turns out this guy was a Penn State professor of agronomy who specialized in turf. He began bringing students on field trips in buses to take a look at the good, the bad, and the ugly in lawns. Guess whose lawn was the "bad and ugly." You got it – yours truly. He used my lawn to point out the weeds that they were studying. He also filmed it for a Penn State PBS *Lawn Doctor* show he had on local TV. I told him if my house was ever identifiable on the show, I would sue him – after I burned his house down.

There is some good news about this tale, however. He started a lawn service firm, and I became a customer. Soon my lawn looked as good as his – almost.

Life Lesson 52 comes from this experience.

Life Lesson 52: Thou shall not covet thy neighbor's grass.

I guess the King James' edition of the Bible lost the original wording in translation.

The Composition of the 'Hood

The 'hood consisted of three houses on a cul-de-sac and one adjoining property behind two of the houses. The residents were four young families. We all moved in at approximately the same time. The first family was the Hughes. Their patriarch, Art, was an administrator in the Agriculture College at Penn State, and his wife was a schoolteacher. They had twin boys, one year younger than our son.

The second family was the Watsons. As I mentioned, the husband, Tom, was a professor of Turf at Penn State, and his wife was a schoolteacher. They had one son who was a couple of years younger than our son.

The third family was the Schaffers. The husband, Gary, was a coach at Penn State, and (yep, you are correct) the wife was a schoolteacher. They had two sons who were several years younger than our son.

And the Queen and I were the fourth family. I was a spook software weenie at HRB Singer, and coincidentally, at that time, the Queen was a schoolteacher. We had one son. Are you seeing a pattern here?

We were so overflowing with schoolteachers and boys that we could have started our own teachers' union and Little League team.

Here's a riddle for you. How many neighbors does it take to start a party? The answer is one if he strolls across the neighborhood lawns carrying a six-pack of beer. (At the time it was Old Milwaukee, which was all we could afford.) This was the start of many weekends going bad.

Our motto became Life Lesson 53.

Life Lesson 53: Life is just a bowl of pretzels. Grab a beer!

We all soon became very good friends and spent a lot of time together, and we had some great adventures.

The Coach also taught scuba diving at Penn State and had access to the Penn State Natatorium. Therefore, on many Sunday mornings, when the Natatorium was closed, all four families would gather at the Nat and spend the morning frolicking in the pool. This was followed by brunch at someone's house, and then it was watching football and eating "take-out" from Susie Wong's Chinese restaurant. Great way to spend a Sunday relaxing.

Our secondary motto became Life Lesson 54.

Life Lesson 54: Enjoy the weekend because Monday comes quicker than lager turns to pee.

We also relished playing practical jokes on each other. Probably the best was when Art Hughes got a permit to cut firewood on the state game lands. He found a perfect fourteen-foot log that could be used as a basketball pole for his driveway, and his boys were ecstatic. He brought the pole home and left it lying in his driveway. The family had to go out after that, and while they were away, the other three neighbors hid the pole behind one of our houses and then took pieces of firewood, which were each approximately two feet in length, and laid them end-to-end where he had placed the pole. In between the logs, we scattered wood shavings. When he came home, he went absolutely bat-shit. He called us every name under the sun. Meanwhile, we took the boys behind the house, showed them the pole, and explained what we had done. They thought it was funny. However, Art never forgave us the entire time they lived on Abbey Place.

I hasten back to repeat Life Lesson 15.

Life Lesson 15: Some people can't take a joke.

Our boys grew up riding their Big Wheels around the cul-de-sac. On July 4, 1976, the 200th anniversary of the United States, we had a neighborhood parade with flags and Big Wheels and boys. The parents sat on the curb eating the All-American Breakfast, a bowl of Cheerios floating in Budweiser. Is this a great country or what?

Two of the neighbors, the Coach and Dr. Turf, shared the same birthdate. On their mutual 50th birthday, three of the couples headed to the US Virgin Islands to celebrate for a week.

We spent the week frolicking in the sand, sightseeing, drinking rum concoctions, and partying. We even invited some of the locals to our parties. For example, one evening the pizza delivery driver, Bernadette, decided to abandon her route and join us. Free pizza for all!

We probably weren't the quietest group on the island. On the final day, the Coach and I were sitting in a bar while our wives shopped. We started a conversation with the woman sitting next to us. She asked us where we were staying, and when we told her, she said, "Oh, you're the noisy bastards." That was us – goodwill ambassadors to the world.

We also vacationed together. On one trip to Virginia Beach, the four couples rented a house and spent a week on the beach. This included crabbing and fishing for spot, a saltwater fish. We used frozen squid for bait. Unfortunately, Art Hughes forgot to take the bait out of the trunk of his ancient four-door Thunderbird, and it baked there in the sun for several days. They ended up driving home with all the windows down and their heads hanging out of the windows, just like dogs do in a car. He eventually sold the car – I'm not sure if it was due to the fragrance or because some guy yelled at him "quit polluting the Earth." (The T-Bird burned oil and resembled a black cloud moving down the highway.)

In spite of the environment we created, our boys grew up to be solid citizens. Altogether, we have a corporate general counsel, an MD, a financial advisor, a VP of Marketing for a sports apparel company, a proposal manager for an international elevator company, and a home-renewal contractor. All are married and have children of their own.

The Abbey Place experience was unique. We four families grew up together and came to realize what Atal Bihari Vajpayee, former Prime Minister of India, said in Life Lesson 55.

Life Lesson 55: You can't pick your neighbors, but you can choose your friends.

This was a time when we chose our neighbors as friends.

Friends in All Places

During our 53 WONDERFUL years of marriage, we have lived in State College (19 years), Annapolis, MD (3 years), State College (again for 6 years), Plano, TX (14 years), Sarasota/Lido Beach (10 years), and Longboat Key (less than a year). Everywhere we've lived, we have made some true and unique friends. (Saying "eccentric" wouldn't be polite here, so I chose the euphemism "unique.") By the way, "euphemism" is another $10 word that means "chicken shit way to avoid the truth." Let me run through the cast of characters.

I already covered the State College 'hood, so I'll start with Annapolis, MD.

Babs and Lou Green

We first met Babs and Lou when the Queen was selling real estate in Annapolis. Her previous broker from State College gave her their names and said, "These people are moving from Connecticut to Annapolis. You may not sell them a house, but they're great people and I think you could be friends with them." Lou was a gregarious, Energizer Bunny type of individual who was taking a position as president of a Baltimore spice company. Babs, on the other hand, was not about to trust this new, unknown real estate agent. The Queen did sell them a lot on Maynadier Creek, a tributary of the Severn River, and they built a beautiful house which was about four miles from us.

The Queen's State College broker was right. We did become close friends and shared many experiences over the three years we were in Annapolis, and this friendship continued when we moved back to State College. It turned out Babs and Lou are rabid Penn State fans and attended all the games. When we moved back to State College, they stayed with us on football weekends, and we attended the games together.

They had a 28-foot sailboat which was the source of many adventures. Every time we went somewhere on the boat, Murphy's Law beat the crap out of us.

We had one trip where the wind was calm, the fuel

pump went bad, and I spent the entire distance across the Chesapeake Bay hand-pumping fuel into the engine. On another venture, the engine died on our way home, and Lou swam with the tow rope in his teeth pulling us from the Severn River into the dock at Maynadier Creek.

We enjoyed many weekends on the Eastern Shore in Rock Hall, Maryland, eating crabs at the marina and drinking beer at the Old Ore Inn. The Old Ore Inn was quaint (for lack of a better word). It had peanut shells on the floor, drywall that was taped but not finished, and Buddy, a guitar player who had a rock band that played the local pubs. Buddy took a hankering to the Queen (he called her "Awnrey") and invited us to their gig at a local bar one evening. We went, and when we entered, the band was in the middle of a song when Buddy spotted her, stopped the music, and yelled, "Awnrey!" The Queen was in her glory, being recognized in a dive bar on the Eastern Shore. She gave her little Queenie wave like Queen Elizabeth does.

Meanwhile, I was also recognized. Upon entering, I ran into two employees of mine at our Maryland facility. It turns out that their aunt owned the bar. Small, embarrassing world, ain't it?

That night we had to help break up a fight between two women in the parking lot on our way out. All in the line of duty!

It seems like the girls had a propensity for bringing strangers back to the boat. One time it was two DC police detectives who had investigated the Watergate break-in. You never knew who was going to show up to visit when the two women were on the loose.

We also made multiple sailing vacations to the US

Virgin Islands, the British Virgin Islands, Grenada, and other Caribbean Islands. Most of the time we bare-boated. Louie was an alumnus of the US Coast Guard, so he professed a deep knowledge of sailing. Beware of what US Coast Guard guys tell you. For these trips we usually rented a sailboat about 50 feet in length. Of course, we had minor accidents, but that's what insurance is for.

We also learned to speak the native dialect. For example, one day in British Virgin Gorda we were filling the tanks with fresh water. The native who was helping us started screaming, "Squee-de-hoe! Squee-de-hoe!" We finally figured out he was yelling "Squeeze the hose" to stop the water flow.

Shortly before I retired, Lou retired, and they moved to Crystal Beach, Florida, about an hour and a half away from Sarasota. So we were near and could continue to see each other. In addition, when we purchased the fish camp in State College, we were able to continue with the four of us getting together for football games.

The Texas Friends

When we moved to Texas in 1994, we really knew no one outside of my work environment. Not to worry. Texans are the friendliest people in the world, and we soon met one neighbor who introduced us to their friendship circle. And what a circle it was.

Texas is a whole 'nother country.

First of all, everybody goes by two names – Jim Bob, Betty Jane, Carolyn Sue, Bobby Ray, Bobby Paul, etc. It's a way of life. In fact, we have one friend, Jim Bob, whose son's name is Jay, and he goes by Jay Bob. Their dog's name is Scooter —you got it, Scooter Bob.

Second, everybody is a college football fanatic. You either root for Texas, Texas A&M, Oklahoma, or Oklahoma State. And it's serious shit. As an example, one set of our friends are Texas fans and another set are Oklahoma fans. One year, the Texas friends drove to the Red River Shootout, the big Texas-Oklahoma game held at the Cotton Bowl, and they took our Oklahoma friends with them to the game. At half time Oklahoma was drumming Texas badly, so the Texas friends announced, "We're going home, and you can find your own way back to Plano." And they left. Our Oklahoma friends ended up taking a bus back to Plano. Didn't I tell you football is serious shit?

Third, the Mexican food in Texas is outstanding, and the chicken-fried steak is to die for. We were also introduced to greens (collard greens, mustard greens, turnip greens, chard, kale, etc.), black-eyed peas, catfish, and fried pies. The southern boys know how to eat.

Fourth, Texas women are the prettiest in the world. No ifs, ands, or buts. Case closed. Of course, Dallas is known for its big blonde hair, big diamonds, and big breasts (all natural, I'm sure).

Regarding the topic of natural endowments, one evening a female Texas friend had been overserved and was returning from the ladies' room with the other women in our group. When they walked past the bar, a blonde with obviously enhanced, perky, full breasts was sitting there with a man. Our friend walked up to her, flicked her finger on the blonde's chest, and said, "How much did you pay for those puppies?" The other women escorted her quickly out of the bar before Wrestlemania II began. Gotta love those Texans!

But the number one thing I love about Texas is the attitude. Everything in Texas is bigger, prettier, smarter, you name it, than any other place in the world. Swagger rules. Don't give me no New York City shit, I'm from Texas.

When I retired and we decided to move to Florida, our friends in Texas couldn't understand it. They were very serious when they said, "How could you leave here where all your friends are and go somewhere that you don't know anyone?" Well, we appreciate how they felt about us, but basically, we were looking for a warmer climate and living on the water – two things Texas couldn't offer.

Our Condo Friends on Lido Beach

I've already talked about the condo on Lido Beach, so I won't repeat myself. However, while we were there, we did make some good friends, people that we enjoyed spending time with. For the most part, at this stage in our lives, we just go out to dinner with friends. We are well beyond the party-party-party era.

I will end this chapter with what I believe are the best lessons about friends.

Life Lesson 56: Friends are like condoms: they protect you when things get hard.

I also like Life Lesson 57 which is a popular quote.

Life Lesson 57: Good friends don't let you do stupid things... alone.

And on a more serious vein, there is Life Lesson 58.

Life Lesson 58: In the end, your health will fail you, your memory will fail you, and your energy will fail you. Your friends will remain friends.

The Queen and I are thankful for the friends we have made and maintained over the years. They share our experiences and are an important part of our lives.

Chapter 17: Aging

According to the actress Bette Davis, the primary message about aging is Life Lesson 59.

Life Lesson 59: Old age isn't for sissies.

Throughout our lives we are fed the propaganda of the "Golden Years" until we drink the Kool-Aid and believe it. The promise is a vibrant, sunny, and happy life. And what really lies in store? Aches, pains, maladies, nose and ear hair accompanied by the loss of hair on the top of your head, stiffness where you don't want it and lack of stiffness where you do want it, hearing difficulties, shrinking, forgetfulness, and a general slowing-down.

What happened to my gold? "Aging gracefully" is both an oxymoron and a myth. If you were a pipe, you'd be rusting.

For those of you who point out the positive aspect of time, i.e., time heals all wounds, I suggest Life Lesson 60 from Lucille Harper.

Life Lesson 60: Time is a great healer but a poor beautician.

And age sneaks up on you. Perhaps I can help by identifying some warning signals that you are getting old.

1. Everyone you meet calls you "sir."

2. A successful meal is one where you don't spill something on your clothes.

3. You leave the zipper on your pants down more than three times a day.

4. Shirt buttons become difficult to fasten because your fingers don't work like they used to.

5. When the going gets tough, you take a nap.

6. You go to the store and forget (a) why; (b) your glasses, wallet, hearing aids, etc.; (c) where you parked; (d) your wife; (e) all the above.

7. You can remember every word of a song from 1962, but you can't remember why you walked into the kitchen.

8. Some mischievous person, or perhaps an alien, regularly hides your phone, keys, and glasses.

9. You are two inches shorter than you were.

10. Your chest moves down closer to your belt, so you wear your pants lower.

11. Time passes by faster and faster each year.

They say age is just a number. OK, but in my case it's a BIG number.

However, getting old sure beats the other option.

The only thing that moves faster as we age is our age. OK, I made that up, but according to *Scientific American*,[x] the sensation that time speeds up as we get older is real. If we engage in novel pursuits (as we do when we are young), we remember the activities later on, and they seem to have lasted longer than the more mundane experiences we have already done. So get out that bucket list of new adventures, carpe diem (Just Do It), and slow down the clock.

A word of caution here. Novel pursuits do not include new injuries or maladies. Time will C-R-A-W-L S-L-O-W-L-Y while you heal and want things to speed up.

Congregating

When the realization finally hits us that we are becoming our parents, what do we do? Okay, you're ahead of me here. We stick together in senior groups.

1. We move into 55-and-older developments/communities which abound with social events, e.g., TGIF get-togethers, Sip and Stroll street parties, TV event parties (Super Bowl, Kentucky Derby, etc.), holiday parties, wakes, etc. The communities also organize group activities such as exercise classes, bus trips, hikes, knitting, pickle ball, and book clubs. Busy, busy, busy!

2. We dine out with friends who are our mirror images, and the number-one conversation topics are our ailments, maladies, medical procedures, etc. You can't beat a good fried or red-meat meal

while discussing IBS, heart problems, choles-
terol, or erectile dysfunction.

3. If we aren't getting enough activity from the first
   two actions above, we join a country club where
   we can golf, play tennis, and socialize with a new
   group of our peers.

4. We go on cruises with thousands of "new friends"
   who look and act just like our "old friends," and
   we eat and drink our way around the world. Bon
   voyage, Chunky!

Exercise

Life Lesson 61 summarizes the need for total exercise.

**Life Lesson 61: As we age, regular
exercise becomes more and more
important. You need to exercise
your body, mind, and laughter.
Remember: It's use it or lose it.**

Relative to the body, my doctors tell me that exercise
is the best medicine for Parkinson's Disease, and it is
more important than the myriad of expensive prescriptions that I take to slow down progression of the disease.

In terms of exercising the mind, word games, Sudoku,
crossword puzzles, remembering your children's names,
etc. keep you going.

And what about laughter? Life Lesson 62 from Mary
Pettibone Poole tells us why.

Life Lesson 62: He who laughs lasts.

And I believe in Life lesson #63.

Life Lesson 63: Laughter is the best medicine – preventer.

According to the online community Gaiam,[xi] a team of doctors in California have researched the benefits of laughter and found amazing results. Get ready to get your giggle on! Laughter:

1. Lowers blood pressure.

2. Reduces stress hormone levels.

3. Works your abs.

4. Improves cardiac health – especially for those who are incapable of doing other physical activity due to injury or illness. It burns a similar number of calories per hour as walking at a slow to moderate pace. This puts new meaning to the phrase "Laugh your ass off!"

5. Boosts T cells.

6. Triggers the release of endorphins.

7. Produces a general sense of well-being – people who have a positive outlook on life tend to fight diseases better than people who tend to be more negative. So smile, laugh, and live longer!

Drug Stores

The days of the mom-and-pop drug stores on the corner are over, replaced by a CVS or a Walgreens On Every Corner. If you don't like your CVS, cross the street to the next one. According to my research assistant, Mr. Google, there are more CVS and Walgreens in the United States than there are McDonald's. Baby Boomers rule!

A Final Note on Aging

Life Lesson 64 characterizes how we feel.

Life Lesson 64: Getting old is the opposite of having sex: when you have sex, you feel good near the end.

On this cheery note, let's move on to Travel.

Chapter 18:
Travel

There are three reasons to travel:

1. You have to go somewhere (business travel, weddings, etc.);

2. You want to go somewhere (vacations, visit friends, etc.); or

1. You need to get away (prison escapee, Witness Protection Program, snowbird, etc.).

Business Travel

During my career, the travel was predominantly business. Throughout the final fourteen years, I was located in Dallas, most of my customers were in DC, corporate headquarters were in the Boston area, our business encompassed fourteen sites in the United States, and we had employees supporting a number of customer sites around the world.

As a result, I spent most of my time on the road (or more precisely, in the air). I accumulated almost six million miles with American Airlines. Therefore, the Executive Platinum desk at American was attentive. For example, when the Queen called them to arrange personal travel, they actually asked her, "Where would Your Royal Highness like to go today?" She said "HUH?" and the agent said, "I'm looking at your husband's activity screen, and to American, you are The Royal Highness. Now where would Her Highness like to go today?" She took it in stride as any monarch should do.

And in the Admiral's Club at Dulles Airport, the girls on the desk told her, "We see more of your husband than you do." That didn't go over as well as the Royal Highness remark did, but it was the truthiness.

I once told my staff that we would implement the "two-row rule": none of them should be sitting within two rows of me on the plane. I liked to use flight time to catch up on paperwork (or whatever the electronic equivalent is called). They ignored me. I guess that as former staff they can now sit anywhere they want. Before you get offended and burn the book, I'm just pulling your chain. I just upped their quotas to get even.

On one particular Friday afternoon, I was seated on a plane at Dulles Airport waiting to fly to Dallas with my head buried in a newspaper. A young man sat down next to me and asked the time. When I told him, he said, "That voice... I recognize that voice from our all-hands meetings. You're Mike Keebaugh!" When I said that I was, he said, "I work for you, and now I have two and a half hours of your undivided attention." Mon Dieu! I do credit him with taking full advantage of the opportunity.

On many of my overseas trips, the Queen was able to accompany me (by eating into the six million miles to purchase first-class tickets). This was her "vacation" while I worked.

One place she couldn't tag along was Adak, Alaska.

Early in my career, I often supported deployment of equipment that we had developed, and one of the sites was on Adak, the next-to-last island on the Aleutian chain. If Sarah Palin can see Russia from her backyard, people on Adak can pass them the Grey Poupon mustard.

The only way to get to Adak was on Reeves' Aleutian Airlines, and they flew a round trip twice a week. While I was there, our two-year-old son got an extremely high temperature and was hospitalized. The doctor called me and said that I'd better come home. I explained where I was and the delay in waiting for Reeves' day to fly, and he still said to come home. Several days later, when I walked into Todd's hospital room, he was sitting up in bed and said, "Hi, Dad."

When I talked to the doctor, he pulled me aside and said, "Look, I was in the Navy in World War II. I know where Adak is. What did you do to piss off your company that they sent you there?"

Great Harbour Cay

While we were living in Texas, we bought into a self-managed timeshare house on Great Harbour Cay (GHC) in the Bahama Islands. This probably raises two questions – What is a self-managed timeshare house? And what is Great Harbour Cay?

First, a group of eight couples, all of whom were either friends or relatives of Jim, one of the owners, purchased a house on the beach. Some couples had two shares, making the total twelve shares. Thus, one share was equal to four weeks' use during the year. Jim managed the allocation of time and settled conflicts.

Second, GHC is the major island in the north Berry Islands, an island chain with seven miles of beaches, located south of Grand Bahama and Freeport, and north of Nassau. According to the 2010 census, it has a population of 353. In the late '60s, it underwent major development and was a vacation spot for the "stars." That died off in the '70s and was replaced by drug and weapons trafficking in the '80s. However, the island has been quiet since then. There is only one hotel on the island, catering primarily to Bahamians.

There is no commercial air service to GHC, but there is an airport that you can charter into. So what we would do was fill a large cooler with ice and frozen meat purchased at Costco in Plano, TX. We would check it as luggage on the American flight to Fort Lauderdale. (Things were a lot looser then – can you imagine doing this today under TSA monitoring and the airlines' money-grab restrictions on luggage?) The next morning, we would buy one or two weeks (depending on the length of our stay) of groceries, wine, and beer at Publix in Fort Lauderdale and then load the cooler, groceries, alcohol, luggage, and ourselves onto a charter plane that was older and in worse shape than we were for a 100-mile flight to GHC.

Life on GHC was simple, and everything ran on island time (translated as "today, tomorrow, or whenever I get to it"). The organizational model was flat – no layers of bureaucracy here. For example: the Customs Department was one man, Mr. Finley. The arrival team was one man, Conchman. The power company was one man, Shoes, and the plumbing company was one man, Roger.

The grocery store was about one-fourth the size of a

7-Eleven, and most of the time its shelves were empty. The exception was on Saturday when the mail boat from Nassau brought in fresh supplies. There were two places to eat out on the island. The first was a beach "restaurant" that made Guy Fieri's dive bars seem like haute cuisine (hotsy-totsy, fancy-schmantsy), and the other was the Pool Bar, named for the algae-green pool on the property, which also served as the island's mosquito-breeding grounds.

That was it for the excitement on GHC. The rest was relaxing in the serene, beautiful environment. We had a small 21-foot boat which was used for fishing, sightseeing, and getting stuck on sand bars. We also had an ancient Ford Bronco with no headliner and minimal floorboards which was used to get around.

We maintained a "To Do" list of maintenance items for the house, and everyone was expected to work on the items during their stay. One December while the Queen and I were in residence, I noticed that the Bronco's inspection sticker had expired the previous October. I called Jim to find out what I should do. He said I needed to get proof of insurance from the marina store, make sure everything was operational on the vehicle (he emphasized that they were strict, so be certain everything functioned), go to the police station for the inspection, and take all the paperwork and a check to the town offices. There was only one slight problem – nothing on the vehicle worked. So I spent several days fixing the windshield wipers, brake lights, turn signals, etc. When I went to the police station in my refurbished vehicle, I was told it was closed for Christmas week. I should come back in two days.

Two days later, I drove to the police station, which was manned by a large, native officer who was clearly hung over from the previous night's police holiday party. He spent a half-hour filling out paperwork by hand (none of them fancy computers on GHC), and then said, "OK, it's time for the inspection. Does everything work?" I said yes, and he said, "Inspection passed."

There are two lessons I learned here.

Life Lesson 65: Timing is everything.

If you catch someone when they are preoccupied or indisposed, they often relax the rules for the sake of convenience.

And the old Boy Scout motto is Life Lesson 66.

Life Lesson 66: Be Prepared.

If you plan and prepare for the worst case, more often than not, it doesn't happen – and if it does, you are ready.

Eventually, we owners tired of the difficulties in getting to the island, supply logistics, and maintenance issues, and we sold the house. However, we have many fond memories of GHC.

Reader Check – If you are still loving it, tweet me at @TheRealMarkTwain. If you are still there but you're not sure why, tweet me at @GuttingItOut. If you gave up, no tweet is necessary, you wimp.

Now let's look at our travel in the post-retirement years.

Chapter 19:
Post-Retirement Travel
– The Early Years

After I retired in 2009, the Queen and I became interested in travel. Since we didn't qualify to "join the Navy and see the world," we enlisted travel agencies or arranged it ourselves. We decided to focus on four things:

1. See America – For forty-plus years, I spent considerable (a euphemism for excessive) time crisscrossing the United States at 30,000 – 33,000 feet. Unless you are Rod Sterling living in the Twilight Zone, you can't get a picture of the land or a feeling for the people through an airplane window (where Rod met weird little creatures on the plane's wings). You need to experience it at the ground level – up close and personal. And domestic travel is easier than foreign travel. As Dave Barry points out, "The major advantage of domestic travel is that, with a few exceptions such as Miami, most domestic locations are conveniently situated right here in the United States."

2. See the places that we have read about and where history was made. We were particularly interested in the European countries.

3. Go to the forbidden places. Throughout my career, I worked in a classified security environment. There was a list of countries that I couldn't visit because of the clearances I held. Now we are free to explore. Let's visit the Commies!

1. Fly-fish the famous streams and rivers of the US.

We put some restrictions and filters on our travel:

1. We will not book trips on the mega-passenger cruise ships. Sharing an adventure with 3,000 to 4,000 of your new best friends from Des Moines, Iowa or Berkley Springs, West Virginia doesn't appeal to us. We decided that any cruise we took would accommodate a maximum of 100 or so.

2. A substantial portion of the trip must have accommodations at the four-star and higher levels. Remember, I am travelling with the Queen, and this is her minimum standard.

3. We will visit no war zones or high-risk areas. We are too damned old to become hostages.

4. We will limit our travel to a maximum number of days-away for each trip. The Queen wanted this to be three weeks. I insisted on one week. After considerable dialogue, we compromised on three weeks.

Adventures and Misadventures

In our travels, we have uncovered a hidden talent for creating chaos out of plans. If you are old enough to remember Al Capp's L'il Abner comic strip, there was a character named Joe Btfsplk who was the world's worst jinx. He walked around with a dark rain cloud hovering over his head, and he brought misfortune to everyone in proximity. Well, meet Joe's son, yours truly, Mike Btfsplk. It seems that every trip we take becomes an adventure, which is "an unusual and exciting, typically hazardous experience or activity" according to the online dictionary. That's us – Mr. and Mrs. Hazardous.

Let's talk some Travel Life Lessons here.

Life Lesson 67: If something can go wrong, it will.

This is known as Murphy's Law. There is considerable controversy about who the real Murphy was. My theory is that it was Richard Nixon during the Watergate caper. The British also refer to this as Sod's Law, and Finagle's Law adds the phrase "at the worst possible time."

If we take Life Lesson 67 to the next level, we get Life Lesson 68.

Life Lesson 68: Murphy was an optimist.

There is even more controversy about who said this, so I won't go there. Anyhow, where I was headed is that the Queen and I have no such thing as an ordinary trip;

we have adventures. The American author Mercedes Lackey sums up an adventure as "I guess that's what you call it when everybody comes back alive."

And there is a third Life Lesson which is a corollary to Murphy's Law.

Life Lesson 69: Plan B is used more often than Plan A.

No matter how well you plan, shit happens, and your plan goes down the toity. Improvisation rules, dude! Unfortunately, this phenomenon becomes the norm when flying in and out of State College, PA. Let me give you just one example.

The flight from State College to Philadelphia on American Airlines (old USAir, older Allegheny Air) has a 30-minute flight time. On a recent flight where we were connecting to Atlanta, after 15 minutes in the air, the pilot announced that we had "an electrical problem" and needed to return to State College. Wait a minute – if you're halfway between your starting point and destination, why not go to where you are supposed to be??? Shortly after, he said we were going to Harrisburg since the runway was longer (later we found out that the actual reason was that Harrisburg is where the mechanics are). We landed and were escorted by a parade of fire trucks and emergency vehicles with lights flashing and sirens blaring – talk about a confidence builder!!

Since there were no spare planes at the inn, the plan was to send us to Philadelphia on a bus. During my career, in an attempt to curb the Queen's spending habits, I repeatedly told her that if she continued at her pace, we would spend retirement traveling on a Greyhound bus. See? I was right all along!

[Note to Reader – Don't attempt to use the potty on a bus at highway speeds unless you are a trained gymnast. – End Note]

After a three-hour bus ride, we arrived at the Philadelphia Airport and got booked on a much later flight. (Our original flight was gone, gone, gone.) We arrived at Atlanta and went directly to our event (smelly, with luggage, and two hours late). Our total travel time was twelve hours-plus. Thankfully, I am not a Type A+ person!!

The Travel Blogs

When we began our retiree travel, I started chronicling the adventures in a series of emails that recorded our experiences along the trip, and I sent them out to family and friends. They described the day-to-day misadventures, the "cultural tours" from the perspective of a poor old country boy, and life with the Queen. The response to the blogs was positive, with requests to subscribe, and that encouraged me to continue. Today, I have almost 100 on the highly sought-after subscription list, and the majority who get the blogs forward them to one or more family or friends. Hardly best-seller communications, but the price is right.

As I mentioned in PART I, the feedback from the blog recipients is one of the reasons I decided to write a book. The readers enjoyed the epistles and encouraged me to "write a book." Therefore, you have them to blame.

And if it doesn't work out, I still have my day job. Wait

a minute – what the hell am I talking about? I don't have a day job; I'm retired.

So this chapter and the next summarize our eleven years of post-retirement travel misadventures, not from a travel-guide perspective which focuses on places to go and see, but rather as a discussion and examination of our "adventures" and the lessons learned.

I confess that "cultural osmosis" is not my strong point. As a Type A+ person, I have a limit on how many cathedrals, paintings, museums, and structures that I can absorb before my mind drops out, so I probably will shortchange some esoteric, artistic aspects (I probably was daydreaming while the guide lectured). I have an internal Culture-O-Meter that shows when I have maxed out on cultural absorption and the "tank is full" light comes on, preventing further input (remember my Appalachian small-town roots). When this happens, my eyes glaze over and my brain goes into neutral.

Once again, my lawyer insists that I remind you: "The names have been changed to protect my butt."

By the way, don't you just love the myriad of CYA (cover your ass) disclaimers that are required in our communications today? For example:

1. Medical Ads – If you have ever had toenail fungus or are allergic to water or have a fear of clowns, consult your doctor before taking Panacea. Rare but serious side effects may include howling at the moon, getting the munchies for cat food, etc.

2. ED Ads – Contact your doctor or seek emergency

medical attention if your erection is painful or lasts longer than four hours. (Now be honest. If this happens, won't you be too busy doing other things to call your doctor?)

3. Coupons – Certain restrictions may apply (followed by a long paragraph of unreadable fine print excluding every item and brand that you desire).

But again, I digress, which is common for geezers of my age. Let's move on to the travel.

The Great American Road Trip

In August 2009, we began the Great American Road Trip. Unfortunately, the blogs from this excursion were lost in my transition from Dell/BlackBerry to Apple, an epiphanic transition (Aha moment) to the "dark side" in 2013, so I'll reconstruct the narrative (a writing term that means "make up stuff").

We packed up the car (at this time, a BMW sedan) with the Queen, Sapphire (our twelve-year-old Bichon Frise), the royal luggage, my fishing gear, and me, and headed out from Florida across America – 38 days, 8,007 miles, 28 states and ZERO speeding tickets. However, we did develop two sore butts.

We started in Pennsylvania and Ohio visiting family and friends. Then the adventure began!

We entered the heart of America, the great Midwest, and crossed Indiana (the Hoser State – whoops, typo – I mean Hoosier State). By the way, do you know what a Hoosier is? Don't feel bad, neither do the Indianaites.

There are multiple theories about an Anglo-Saxon word meaning hill, a contractor named Hoosier who hired crews from Indiana, hence Hoosier's men, and an Indian word for corn (hoosa). After passing through the state, my money is on the corn.

The next "drive-through" state was Illinois, which gave us Abe Lincoln, Ronald Reagan, and Al Capone – two log-splitters and a head-splitter. There are two parts to Illinois: Chicago and cornfields.

Finally, Iowa rounds out the Corn Belt triumvirate. The derivation of the name "Iowa" is a daisy chain. The state of Iowa, originally a territory of Wisconsin west of the Mississippi River, was named after the Iowa River. The Iowa River was named after the Iowa Indians who lived in the territory. Their tribal name "Ayuxwa" was spelled by the English as "Ioway." Not coincidentally, "Ayuxwa" means "one who puts to sleep." Therefore, Iowa means the state that puts you to sleep. And as you drive through Iowa, you definitely feel that the name is spot-on!

By the way, Iowa is one of the safest places to live in the US. I guess it's hard to get hurt in a corncob duel. I think that two out of every three people in Florida are from Iowa, although I've never heard of anyone relocating from Florida to Iowa. Wonder why?

We had fun in South Dakota – the Corn Palace (a large arena covered inside and out with colored corn ears, probably imported from Iowa), the Badlands (beautiful, rugged geological structures), Mount Rushmore (no Obama head – YET), the Crazy Horse monument (a work in progress), Wall Drug (the road signs are better than the place), and Sturgis (the mecca of Harley riders).

After purchasing our share of Sturgis paraphernalia, including Harley thongs for the Queen, we headed west to Montana. The name Montana comes from the Spanish word *montaña*, which means "mountainous country." DUH!

We visited Bozeman, MT, where I fished three trout streams – the Yellowstone, the Gallatin, and Hyalite Creek. (Life is good.)

Then we toured Yellowstone and got up close with a buffalo herd who thought they owned the road, and since they were each as large as our car, I agreed.

Life Lesson 70: Hell hath no fury like a bison horned.

Yes, I know the original proverb is "woman scorned," but if one of these large, hairy animals with horns, dripping saliva from its mouth and lacking a sense of humor, ever sticks his nose up to your driver's side window, you'll be cleaning the stains off your seat covers.

We went to Jackson, WY, where we visited Jackson Hole and the Mangy Moose Saloon. (Andrée's picture is still on the wall from a New Year's Eve Party we spent at the Moose many years ago.) P.S. I fished two more streams, the Snake River and Flat Creek.

We drove to Idaho (according to their license plates, home of "Famous Potatoes"), where we spent two days in Last Chance, a town with four structures (an inn/restaurant, a fly shop/inn/restaurant, a standalone fly shop, and a Shell station/grocery/town hall/laundromat – they got it all!). I fished the Henry's Fork for two days while Andrée and Sapphire toured the metropolis (population 286), read, and napped. And yes, there was a sign in our room that read "Fishermen must remove their boots before getting into bed." I was quickly running up a tab in the "You're Gonna Owe Me Big Time" column.

We traveled through Utah (where the license plates say "Live Elevated" – sounds hallucinogenic, but it is more creative than "Famous Potatoes") – past Bryce Canyon, the Red Hills, and Lake Powell, and down to the Grand Canyon (which is unbelievable). Because she was a "senior," the Queen qualified for a lifetime pass to all the National Parks.

We went to Durango, CO and on to Lake City, CO to visit our friends, the Teachers, and to fish two streams, the Gunnison River and Hensen Creek. (It had been four days since I was on a stream, and I was in withdrawal!).

Then we began the scenic part of the tour (NOT!) – across West Texas (sagebrush, barbed wire, and WIND), which made the Iowa cornfields look attractive, and on to Plano where we spent five days with our Texas friends (a great homecoming) and saw many friends at Raytheon.

Now for the *coup de grace* (which, for the not-so-frequent traveler, is a mercy killing and not a Cadillac model). We drove through the Dynamic Duo of states (Mississippi and Louisiana). God truly had a sense of humor when he created them.

For years, we had crossed the USA at thirty thousand feet in a plane, but we hadn't seen things on the ground. This road trip was a fun time, and WE REMAIN MARRIED!!!!!!!!!!!!!

This leads me to a Life Lesson that every prospective couple should use to determine marital compatibility.

Life Lesson 71: If you want a good test of your odds for a successful marriage, take a road trip of at least one month together. Confinement will stir the pot.

This maiden voyage into post-retirement travel convinced us that the Dalai Lama was correct. His quote is Life Lesson 72.

Life Lesson 72: Once a year, go somewhere you've never been before.

So we vowed to do at least one tour every year (two per year if possible), and we have mostly achieved this.

The Great American Road Trip II

The summer of 2010 was primarily spent buying and setting up the fish camp, so technically we missed our yearly vow. OK, call us fickle (bet you haven't used that word recently), but we were busy moving from two locations, buying the remaining "stuff," and installing fixtures, etc. In 2011, we decided to do a repeat of the Great American Road Trip but with a completely new route this time. After leaving from Florida, we visited family in Pennsylvania and Ohio, and headed toward Mackinac Island. Mackinac banned automobiles in 1898, so there are thousands of pedestrians, bicycles, and horse-drawn carriages (with associated horse droppings). In fact, they have guys on bicycles with cans patrolling the streets and cleaning up horse manure. Try putting that on your resume! Maybe Mobile Compost Transfer Technician or Congressional Aide (they do a lot of cleaning up horseshit).

In the season (May through October), there are 10,000 people on the island. In the winter there are 500 (most assuredly 500 winos). Think cold, snow, wind, and hell. By the way, there are seventeen fudge stores on the island. No, I can't explain why.

After two and a half days on the island, we had thousands of pictures of flowers, old buildings, bicycles, and horses' butts. We continued on the Upper Peninsula (home of the Yuppers, as in UP-ers) to Marquette, Michigan. I fished the Yellow Dog River (more like Yeller Dog Crick where I come from).

We left Marquette, MI and headed to Fargo, ND. (Why Fargo? Hell if I know.) Five hundred and five miles through the forests of Michigan, the thousand lakes of Minnesota (we actually only passed 850 lakes), the cheese curls of Wisconsin, and the flats of North Dakota. After nine hours of driving, we arrived in Fargo to find all the hotels/motels/inns/mangers filled. Why? There was a major air show with the Blue Angels there that weekend. Who woulda thunk? Disappointing, since I had my hopes up to meet Marge Gunderson, the pregnant police chief from the movie.

After serious discussions at an elevated level (between the Queen and me) and many phone calls, we got a room at the Wagon Wheel Inn in Valley City, ND, 60 miles west of Fargo. Another adventure!

We checked in and went to the Tavern 41 for dinner. Mistake? No, an experience! The state women's softball championship was in Valley City that weekend, so the place was filled with young ladies, any of whom could have beaten the crap out of me. And apparently softball players do not abstain from alcohol or salty language before the championship games the next day. I learned some new words and combinations of old words that evening. One of the girls went out to dance with a sports bra on and a shirt on over it and came back to the table with a lacy red bra over the outfit? Haven't figured that one out yet.

The highlight of the evening was our waitress, a young blonde who was falling out of her "waitress outfit" (short shorts and a vee-neck t-shirt). She introduced herself as "Hi, I'm Flossie, and I'm drunk!" She explained that she was not supposed to work that night and thus had been drinking there at the bar all afternoon. Then she had been called into duty due to the large crowd. In other words, she was "snockered." She sat down at each table to take orders because she couldn't write and balance at the same time. (Remember, alcohol doesn't make you fat, it makes you lean... lean against tables, chairs, and walls.) I learned more about hair extensions from her that evening than I ever needed to know. I'm sure the softball players felt the same.

She made the Queen some potent vodka tonics that created "a lot of giggles" on our way back to the room. From the Queen, not the waitress.

When it was time to pay the bill for multiple beers, vodka tonics, sandwiches, and a pizza, she was busy, seated at a table, chatting with customers. Two construction workers staying at the motel offered to help and yelled to her, asking what we owed. She yelled back,

"Twenty dollars!" I said it was more, but she insisted. I left her a large tip so she can buy a warmer top to protect her chest in the harsh winters of North Dakota and gas for her car to get to the AA meetings.

The next morning, we went to Fort Smith, MT, which is light years away from the 21st century. Fort Smith is below the Yellowtail Dam, which forms the Big Horn River, a world-class trout stream.

To get to the Big Horn, you must drive 45 miles onto the Crow Indian Reservation. By the way, BYOB because no firewater is sold on the reservation.

According to the "stressed-out" Queen (that should probably be ALL CAPS), Fort Smith is two steps down from Last Chance, ID, where we stayed two years ago. It has three fly shops (all of which have either cabins or trailers for lodging), a post office/laundromat (Sue's Soapbox), a market (mini mini mini 7-Eleven), and a church (those heathens in Last Chance didn't have a church). What it doesn't have (for the whiners) is cell phone coverage or hair dryers in the lodges. This made two places we stayed in without hair dryers if you count the Wagon Wheel Inn in Valley City, ND. I'm in deep doo-doo here. The "You're Gonna Owe Me Big Time" column was building once again.

I will admit that our cabin was "rustic," maybe a half of one star out of five. The roof of the porch had blown off and had not been replaced, and the furniture was "dated." There were no restaurants on the reservation, but the owner cooked for the guests (if you count buying Costco lasagna and heating it up as cooking).

The Big Horn is a great river. The trout are a minimum of 14 to 15 inches and go to over 20. I went on a float trip with a guide, and since it was a slow day in Fort Smith, the Queen agreed to come along on the boat to "sightsee." Of course, there are no ladies' facilities on the trip, so she spent eleven hours worrying (and crossing her legs).

I caught some great fish and lost some monsters. (Have you heard this one before?) Andrée was a great sport and met some new friends. She chain-smoked Camels with Gail who ran the fly shop, her new FFBFF (fly fishing best friend forever), and hugged all the guys in our lodge, as well as our guide, as we left.

Even though she had the time of her life, I don't think she will join me next year – ???

We also visited the Little Big Horn Battlefield. Impressive. Unfortunately, Custer had bad intel. General George could have used a Raytheon system.

The Wagon Wheel and Fort Smith really cost me in paybacks. Our next stop was the Rainbow Lodge, a dude ranch on the Gallatin River at the Big Sky Resort. They have three hair dryers per room. Then we traveled to Jackson, Wyoming where we stayed at the Wort Hotel, and I fished Snake and the Gros Ventre (named for an Indian tribe and which translates to "big belly") Rivers. The accommodations at our last two stops ameliorated the Fort Smith whining. From there it was time to head home with a new perspective on traveling captured in Life Lesson 73.

Life Lesson 73: The best way to expand your horizons is by expanding your horizons.

If you expand your physical horizons by traveling, you will expand your mental horizons by seeing and learning.

The Great American Road Trip II was 5,800 miles long. It took 27 days and 108 pit stops. Again, no speeding tickets.

Given the month of travel, I offer this view of He/She Traveling:

1. Packing – She: "I need choices. We should pack many bags." – He: "I would prefer clean underwear every day if possible."

2. Driving position – He: "Keep right, pass left only." – She: Left Lane Lucy.

3. Wine – She: "A Pinot Noir with a 95 or better *Wine Spectator* rating." – He: "Red."

4. Hotel Breakfast – She: "Yogurt and Hard-Boiled Eggs." – He: "Sausage gravy over waffles."

5. Hotel planning – She: Internet research with ratings and calls for reservations. – He: "Well, it's 6 PM. Let's see what's at the next exit."

6. Hotel needs – She: Suites, foo-foo soaps, and hair dryer. – He: Refrigerator for beer.

7. Evening meal – She: Presentation, Ambience, and Veggies. – He: "MEAT."

Let me remind you of Life Lesson 26.

Life Lesson 26: Opposites attract, then collide.

The Queen's World Tour of the Canadian Rockies

In 2012, we did the Queen's World Tour, a trip by railroad through the Canadian Rockies (my loose definition of "world" is "non-domestic"). Our journey started in Vancouver, which is locally known as RainCouver in the Great Wet North. (You figure it out. It rains about 160 days out of the year.) We also spent time in Victoria, which is the capital city of the province of British Columbia. This included a one-and-a-half-hour ride (EACH WAY!!!!) on a ferry that carried 2,100 people, mostly screaming, obnoxious kids.

Then we got on the Rocky Mountain train for a two-day rail trip to Banff, a picturesque leg of the excursion with extensive wildlife along the way. (Some of it was off the train.)

After touring Banff, we traveled by car to Jasper, where the lawn of our cabin was mowed by an elk (honest). On the way, we went to the Columbia Icefield, and guess who went out on the glacier wearing open-weave sandals? Queens do not wear Uggs or hiking boots like everyone else! From there we traveled to Lake Louise. What a beautiful place, with the turquoise mineral water lake, the mountains, the overhanging glaciers, and the Asian tourists who are stealthily invading Canada in buses. **[Note to Stephen King – How about "Attack of the Asian**

Tourists (Pearl Harbor II)" as the theme/title for a book? – End
Note]

Our final stop on the tour was Calgary, where absolutely nothing memorable occurred. When the Stampede isn't on in town, it reminds you of Detroit.

The Canadian trip was a learning experience about our neighbors to the north. Prior to this, we had little knowledge of the Canucks. Our limited view was that Canada is a large, cold country to the north with an English Queen as the head of state, possessing French-speaking citizens (about a fifth of the population), whose main exports are hockey players and cold fronts. We were like the notorious Al Capone who once said, "I don't even know what street Canada is on." We were quite impressed with our Canadian hosts. However, we unfortunately learned that Canada has 123 species of black flies, whose females must feed on blood to lay their eggs. For your information, male black flies don't bite and are rarely seen, similar to male Canadians.

Canada's primary issue is given in Life Lesson 74.

Life Lesson 74: Canada's major problem is geographical. It is located in a bad neighborhood: next to the United States.

The Attack of the Love Bugs

On our trip home from State College to Sarasota in mid-May, we had an encounter with thousands of mating love bugs, aka honeymoon flies (a Florida "must-see").

After mating, matured pairs remain together (the male love bug dies and is dragged around by the female until she lays her eggs) for up to several days. While joined together, they darken the skies, seek out moving cars and splatter on the car's windshield and front end until the driver loses visibility. If not cleaned quickly, they will destroy the paint. **[Note to Stephen King – Here's another possible winner. "The Attack of the Love Bugs" could have potential as a topic for your next thriller. Maybe you could do an "Attack" series of books. If you are interested, give me a call to discuss. If not, I'll check with Carl Hiaasen about it in one of his Florida "Weirdo" series of books. – End Note]**

The Royal Anniversary Tour

For our 40th wedding anniversary, I gave Andrée a trip to Italy. AND, in 2013 we were on our way!!! If you want to be picky about it (and she does), our 40th was actually six years before, in 2007, but, well, this retirement thing has been hectic, and we just got around to it.

For you shut-ins out there in Readerland, Italy is that boot-shaped country in the Mediterranean known for its pasta, wine, and Mafia (just kidding, Mr. Soprano). The people speak a language characterized by shouting (maybe hearing difficulties are part of their genetic makeup) and hand-waving. And Italy is the only country is the world where "oogling" girls, catcalls, and pinching butts are politically correct.

At the end of May we left for France and Italy – the Royal Anniversary Tour 2013. We started with two days in Nice, France, and Monte Carlo. Perhaps France was best characterized by film director Billy Wilder, who said,

"France is the only country where the money falls apart and you can't tear the toilet paper." Take that, you smug, nose-in-the-air, condescending, frog-eating Frenchies! Easy there, Mike. Get back on point.

Then we boarded *Le Ponant* (which is French for "seasick"), a four-deck, three-masted, 289-foot sailing ship and visited the Italian islands. The tour was unique because our boat could get into the small islands that a mega-cruise ship couldn't, including Elba (Napoleon's home away from home), Corsica, Ponza, Lipari, Stromboli (a live volcano which erupted after dark), Sicily (land of the Godfather), and the Amalfi Coast. We ended up in Malta after a night from hell, being literally tossed about our cabin when we went through the Strait of Sicily), and we had the literal black-and-blue marks to prove it.

Thus ended the sea tour, and we began the land portion.

Plan A for the land tour was simple – fly from Malta at 1:30 PM to Rome and connect to Naples (Napoli to you Eyetalians). But a Swissair plane lost its landing gear in Rome and dug into the runway surface, taking out a runway. Then add that another runway was closed for paving. This left one runway open. Can you spell DELAY? We boarded our plane at 4 and sat on the ground awaiting clearance until 5:30. We landed in Rome and waited 45 minutes for a stairway. (Maybe they didn't know we were coming?) I now understand why the Italians have NEVER won a war. Of course, our flight to Naples was cancelled, so here we were – no luggage, no flight, no staff to help. There were "service" lines of shouting, pushing, hand-waving Italians. And the service employees were effectively "on strike" (Notta my problem). By the way, the Alitalia planes do not have hair under the wings, just the flight attendants. Finally, we retrieved our luggage, got on a train to Rome Central, then Naples, and made our hotel by 1:30 AM.

The remainder of the tour was on land with drivers and tour guides. We spent a day in Pompeii (Lavaland), three days in Positano (which means "town hanging off a cliff") and Capri (think big French shopping mall), and three days in Rome (magnifico).

Rome was a touring whirlwind with our Guide Nazi, Ornella – twenty-five centuries in 48 hours. Mamma Mia!!! Each day we started with a driver and the Guide Nazi at 9 AM.

The first day was History Day – palaces, obelisks, basilicas, government offices, the Forum, the Coliseum (a bigger stadium than Jerry Jones has in Dallas), the Spanish Steps, the Circus Maximus (picture NASCAR with chariots – seated 300,000). **[Note to Publicist – By the way, how are you doing in negotiations with NASCAR about an advertising sponsorship? – End Note]**

The Guide Nazi was overflowing with data, including dates, mythology, significance, etc., and she wanted to share it and share it and share it.... And shame on you to suggest some other path that deviated from her plan. (If you did, she said OK, then she went ahead down her path.)

I now know all of the emperors, their birthdays, favorite colors, pets' names, and shoe sizes. I was afraid to miss something, or I might fail the RSAT (Rome SAT) which was given at the end of each day. The Queen had to take a remedial night class on mythology.

The second day was Vatican Day... What an experience – the Sistine Chapel, the Basilica of Saint Peter (including the underground tombs of the Popes), and Saint Peter's Square (Piazza). We also squeezed in a visit to the Pantheon (a pagan church which we missed on Day 1). I now know all of the 266 Popes' data (including red slipper sizes).

When the tour ended, the Queen was disappointed – three weeks in Italy and NO ONE pinched her butt (or picked our pockets). To add some excitement for her, I got up the next morning and went shopping for cigarettes (everyone in Italy smokes), a narrow-cut black suit and pointy shoes, some hair gel, "cool" sunglasses, a motor scooter, and a couple of cell phones (they have phones growing out of their ears). Then I went home and offered to pinch her butt (or at least whistle at her and make hand gestures).

Life Lesson 75: If you want precision and structure, go to Germany. If you seek royalty and stoicism, visit England. If you love enthusiasm, disorganization, pasta, and good wine, choose Italy.

The British Isles Tour

In mid-August 2014, we departed State College for Scotland and Ireland. Penn State's opening football game was in Dublin on 30 August, so we decided to make an eighteen-day touring event around it in Scotland and Ireland.

The trip started out as a "goat rope," meaning it was

totally disorganized. In fact, it was a zero on a scale of 1 to 10. We were to leave SC at 5:50 PM, fly to Philly, and leave for Edinburgh at 8:50. So we called a cab to the airport for 4:15. When he didn't show by 4:30, we called again – answer: 10 minutes out. He finally arrived at 4:50, and we were off to University Park Airport. Unfortunately, we got behind a farm tractor (I'm not making this stuff up) and got there way late. No problem – WRONG!

Andrée had purchased Business Class tickets to Edinburgh on USAir in February. That is "purchased" with dollars, not points. It seemed that USAir couldn't count to twelve, the number of Business Class seats, and oversold our seats. Do you wonder about their ability to run an airline? Fortunately, it is not a dangerous business! And now, there was no room at the inn (or on the plane). After 30 minutes with the Platinum desk (I have almost six million miles with American – USAir's parent), and after one hour with the gate agent at Philly, we got Coach Exit Row Seats with the center seat blocked. Did I mention that I was ready to go home at this point?

After the plane was one hour late taking off ("MINOR maintenance problem" – which makes you comfortable with all that water to fly over)! Then all the restrooms became clogged (and all unavailable but one). Some fun, huh?

Then in Edinburgh the baggage belt broke – will the good times never end?

Oh, and the Queen was already peeking under the kilts!

We stayed at Gleneagles Resort Hotel (home of the then-upcoming 2014 Ryder Cup), and we traveled to Saint Andrews and saw the Old Course. It was closed for play, so we were able to walk several holes (I had a birdie and two pars – in my mind). Then we motored, on the wrong side of the road, to Edinburgh (the Scots pronounce the city EdinBrrrr – which is either their brogue or because they freeze their butts off year-round).

We toured Edinburgh Castle (first erected by King David I in the early 1100s, and besieged, destroyed, and reconstructed over the years). From there, one can see the Firth of Forth, which is before Fife. A firth is an estuary. This one is on the Forth River. And Fife is on the other side of the firth. Who's on Firth?

Then we spent the evening at a "whiskey event" and the Military Tattoo. You readers have probably figured out what a "whiskey event" is (drinking Scotch). The Military Tattoo is a display of military music, marching, and theatrics. The Edinburgh one is held nightly for three weeks in August on the Esplanade (another $10 word meaning an open plain used as a field for firing weapons) at the castle. Hard to describe – bands of bagpipes, Zulu dancers, the Queen's Band, Maori tribes from New Zealand, the Trinidad Steel Drum military band, toe dancers, the Royal Marine Band, fireworks, light shows, precision rifle corps, etc. Unfortunately, it began to rain about a half-hour into the two-hour show. (Rain in Scotland? Nae!) And by the end, we were wet and cold. Good thing we had Scotch to warm us up!

The next day we flew Aer Lingus (motto – "We are the Gaelic version of USAir") from Edinburgh to Dublin, Ireland. The wait at Customs was longer than the flight. Then we rented a car and drove, again on the wrong side of the road, to Mount Juliet Manor, a bucolic, charming, beautiful, and wonderful get-away (per the Queen) or an old, overpriced, foo-foo joint (per the Scribe).

In Ireland we visited Waterford (yes, Martha, the crystal place), Cork, Blarney (and kissed the stone), the world's worst roads (the Beara and Kerry Loops), Galway, and Ashford Castle.

Yes, the Queen was finally residing in her castle. Ashford was founded in 1228 and was extended to 26,000 acres in 1852 by its then-owner, Sir Benjamin Lee Guinness (of brewing fame). The rooms have been upgraded over the years. For example, our bathroom was redone in 1584. Just kidding – actually, the bathroom was the nicest of any place we stayed on this trip. They have four pages of famous people who have stayed here and the rooms they stayed in. Unfortunately, no one of note has stayed in Room 328 (our room) – maybe because it is as small as a telephone booth (if you can remember that far back).

We stopped in Cong for a pint at the Crowe's Nest Pub. I asked the barkeep why their menu said "Crowe's" and the mirror above the bar said "Crow's" without an "e." He told me that "Crowe's" is correct, but when they opened and ordered the mirror, it was misspelled. They used it anyway. The bloke next to me said, "Oh my God. I have been drinking in here every day for the last ten years and never noticed." He then said, "You must be a policeman to notice that." I said, "Retired – Chief Inspector Blarney S. Fife." He apparently never watched the *Andy Griffith Show* or heard of the Blarney Stone – because he was way impressed.

At the castle, the Queen went falconing (a new word for what falconers do). The regal huntress was paired with a Harris Hawk named Beckett. She had a blast. Guess what she wanted for Christmas? Fortunately, our condo covenants didn't permit raptors.

We then went to Dublin for touristing and the football game prior to returning to the States.

The Queenie Chianti Tour

2014 was a two-fer year – we did two tours. In late September 2014 we flew to Italy (which is Latin for "grape") for a nineteen-day tour. Along with our friends Shari and Rod, we visited Lake Como, Lake Garda, Verona, Venice, and Florence, followed by a week-long villa stay in a vineyard in Greve (the Chianti region).

The flight to Milan was uneventful. It reminded me of all those FANTASTIC business trips that I miss so much – the aging planes and flight attendants, the great airplane food, the TSA, the crowds, breathing recycled air, and being herded on and off the plane like cattle. Dog gone, those were the good old days.

We arrived in Milan four hours before our friends Rod and Shari did, so we had a fun time people-watching in the International Arrival Area. I observed a collective makeup of (1) people who would flunk a Terrorist Profile test (if that were legal); (2) people who appeared to be arriving from countries with viral outbreaks; (3) people who need seat belt extenders; and (4) people in Japanese tour groups following someone carrying a colored pennant. Maybe I'm just overly sensitive?

We then got our rental car, a VW van, and headed out of the pits and onto the racetrack, aka the A8. There are similarities between driving in Ireland and in Italy.

The roads are winding and narrow and go through every little town, and the cars are too small for real suitcases. There are also differences. In Italy one drives on the right (as opposed to the wrong) side of the road. Also, they don't waste money on speed limit signs because no true Eyetalian believes in speed limits. We were passed (on straights, in blind turns, in towns, in parking lots, etc.) by everything from Ferraris to motorcycles to farm tractors.

The highlight of the drive to Lake Como was when a truck we were following met a large bus in a town where the road was too narrow for them to pass. After the traffic backed up in both directions from this stalemate (do you think a macho Italian male driver will back down?), Super Traffic Man got out of the car behind us, backed everyone up so the truck was in front of the bus (wrong side of the road), motioned us to pass both vehicles (with both my mirrors folded in), and backed the truck out of the turn. I guess he then found a phone booth and changed back into his Clark Kentorrelli outfit.

In Bellagio and Menaggio, we went "touring," riding ferries across the lake, and "wine tasting" (a polite term for imbibing). Note that every Italian town must end in a vowel according to Italian Grammar Rule 32. If not, one adds a vowel, e.g., Milan becomes Milano, Naples becomes Napoli, etc.

Next, we traveled to Sirmione on Lake Garda, an interesting city. We had to drive over a moat and through narrow walking streets (past Italians seated in the roadway who sure as hell weren't moving from the center) into the old city where our hotel was located.

We decided to drive around the lake. Since they don't use traffic lights in towns, we went through about 150 traffic circles, and because the mountains drop straight to the lake, we went through about 25 tunnels, anywhere from several hundred feet to several miles in length. But at least the roads were reasonably wide! We had a chance to tour, i.e., shop, in Limone and Garda del Sole.

Then we began the Killer Vee Tour (Verona, Vicenza, and Venice). We went to Verona, the setting for Shakespeare's *Romeo and Juliet*. We saw "the" balcony where the "wherefore art thou Queenie" dialogue supposedly occurred. We rubbed Juliet's right breast (on her statue, only a B cup) for luck – and we did selfies just like the thousand other tourists.

In Water World (Venice, Italy), we visited the surrounding islands, Murano (the Glass City) and Burano (the Lace City), by water ferries. We got through Murano without any glass purchases by either Queen (Andrée or Shari). **[Note to Ted Dickson – the folks at the Murano factory said to say Hi to you and Carolyn and asked how the chandelier was working out. They hope you are coming back! Sales are down. – End Note]**

We spent a day touring Venice (Venezia). Venice is a "water city" (understatement – kinda like the Nautilus is a "water boat"). It is built on a lagoon off the Adriatic Sea and is purported to have a max elevation of three feet. This must be at low tide since, at high tide, many of the piazzas (city squares) are underwater.

The population of Venice is 270,000, and all but 50 or so are pickpockets. (We escaped without incident.)

Next, we drove to Greve (south of Florence) in the Chianti region. We were renting a villa in the middle of the Tenuta di Nozzole winery about five miles outside

Greve. Great stone house with outstanding views of rolling hills and vines. Is Italy a great country or what?

One can drive in any direction and see grapes, grapes, and grapes! Good to know they won't be running out soon. Several days were spent touring historic Chianti towns and sampling vino rosso. Then we visited Florence and toured the Accademia, which has Michelangelo's famous statue of a well-hung David (post-Goliath) and the Uffizi Gallery, the largest display of Italian paintings in the country. Lots of Madonnas, crucifixions, and Baby Jesus paintings.

We also crossed the Ponte Vecchio bridge, and I was "thrilled" by the gold and diamond stores.

Every day we took road trips within the local area, testing our driving, map-reading, hand-gesturing, and parking skills. (No parking space? – No problemo – Create one.)

Since the Queen was slightly under the weather due to a cold and cough, we spent a day visiting medicos (doctors) and farmacias (pharmacies) in Greve. Ever been treated by an Italian doctor communicating through an interpreter who is a paramedic? Well, the Queen has! Never knew medicine had so much hand-waving involved.

Finally, we relocated to Florence and then headed back to Geezerville.

Travel – The Next Chapter

Wow, that's six years of travel. I'm sure it evokes your own travel memories – the good, the bad, and the ugly. Travel is perhaps best summed up by the travel writer

Paul Theroux, who said, "Travel is glamorous only in retrospect." When you are in the midst of airline delays, traffic jams, lost luggage, searching for a rest stop to pee, no hair dryers in the motel room, etc., it ain't so memorable.

Before we move on, feel free to take a break – grab a sandwich and a beer, walk the dog, relax, and get ready for the further adventures of Mr. and Mrs. Btfsplk.

Chapter 20:
Post-Retirement Travel
– The Second Half

Okay. Before we start, let's have a show of hands if you are ready. Gotcha! Just look around the airport gate area where you are seated. Are people staring weirdly at you because you have your hand in the air? Do they think you are asking to use the restrooms? Are they moving away from you?

Put your hand down, and we'll pick up at travel in 2015.

The Maine-land Tour

This tour included four retirees (the Greens, the Queen, and me) on a fall foliage foray and seafood search to the Moose State, Maine – sorta like *Easy Rider* on Geritol.

Here's a quick quiz on Maine for you Mensa wannabes out there – no peeking!

1. What does Maine have that none of the other 50 states have?

2. What is the state bird of Maine?

3. How many states does Maine border?

4. Were any of the original inhabitants' tribe names pronounceable?

5. What is Maine's capital city?

||
V
|| Scroll down for answers.
V
||
V

Answers:

1. Its name is only one syllable.

2. The mosquito.

3. One – New Hampshire

4. No. The original inhabitants of the territory that is now Maine were Algonquian-speaking Wabanaki peoples including the Passamaquoddy, Maliseet, Androscoggin, and Kennebec. If you think you can pronounce them, give it a go, Mr. Mushmouth.

5. Augusta – Ever hear of it? Bet you answered Portland or Bangor.

If you got all five answers correct, send me $22.00 to cover shipping and handling costs, and I'll send you a Certificate of Merit suitable for framing. But enough dilly-dallying. Let's get back to the Maine-iacs.

Mount up, pardner. In September 2015, we overloaded the Audi Q7, headed northeast and drove to Marlboro, MA, where we had a great dinner with the Queen's golf instructor and his significant other. It was nice to finally see the house the Queen bought for him with the payments from her lessons.

The next day, we drove from MA to NH. When you cross the state line there are two gihugic "no tax" state liquor stores where NH is getting even with Taxachu- setts. The line of cars coming north looks like lemmings headed to the cliffs. So we did our part for the local econ- omy. In Maine, we hit Cabela's (as a warmup for LL Bean) and drove to Portland, where we lunched on raw oysters and lobster rolls. I think I like this state. Then we did a walking tour to test Lou's memory of when he was stationed there in the Coast Guard.

Next, it was off to LL Bean, the mecca for hunting, fishing, and outdoor activities. Fortunately, they ship your purchases, since the Audi was already glutted. Then it was on to Samoset, a resort on the water at Rockland, and of course, a lunch of lobster! After lunch, we golfed. What a magnificent venue.

Then we traveled to Camden for a night at the "hippy dippy" Riverside Inn, an eco-friendly abode with a solar panel roof, sunflower gardens (and maybe other plants?), and Birkenstocks. To avoid hunger, we ate lobsters, oys- ters, and clam chowder. After dinner, it was cigars and drinks at the fire pit behind the motel. Like the charac- ters in Chaucer's *Canterbury Tales*, we met many trav- elers and swapped stories of our adventures. We regaled them with stories of our past sailing adventures (misad- ventures).

Afterward, we spent two days in Bar Harbor, where we continued our "see-sea food" seafood diet (any time we saw seafood on the menu, we ordered it). We had huge lobsters (twice) at the Trenton River Bridge Lobster Pound. Then we toured the Acadia National Park and Cadillac Mountain (our Senior Citizen National Park Pass gained us entry). We also visited another of Lou's past Coast Guard haunts and feasted on Smiling Irish Bastard Pale Ale. Our last stop was Kennebunkport for "Queenly" accommodations on the dock and a day of touristy stuff. My "scenic meter full" light went on.

On the tenth and final day, we began the journey to State College (via Boston to see our grandchildren), in a monsoon for most of the trip.

The Cuban Tour

In early April 2016, we did a bucket list trip to Cuba (Havana and Trinidad) – nine days on a private cultural tour. We wanted to go to Cuba before the travel restrictions were lifted and Havana became Miami South – as it was in the '50s BC (Before Castro). It was a great experience.

The Queen and I joined three other couples from Pennsylvania, a guide, and his assistant for an eight-day cultural visit to Cuba. Since US tourism is not sanctioned, trips must have a learning angle. We learned to drink rum and smoke cigars.

Our guide was an American who went to Cuba years ago to write. His Plan A was to become the next Hemingway. He fell in love with the people and the place, and he began doing tours about ten years ago. When Plan A didn't work out, he went full time to Plan B, the tour business, which was significantly more profitable.

We left Tampa via charter aircraft. After a "false push

off" and delay to balance weight distribution (someone's tiara needed to be moved), the flight was uneventful. At Jose Marti International Airport, we were fortunate and only waited two hours for our luggage (three-plus hours can be experienced since there are only several carts in the whole place).

When we got to Havana, we were amazed. Time travel. A 90-mile trip took us back 57 years. All of the autos are circa mid-1950. The architecture is mostly pre-revolution. Electronics are limited.

Travel was mostly by prearranged "taxis." The most popular were '53/'55/'57 Chevys, '54/'55/'57/'59 Fords, and a few Pontiacs, Buicks, and Mercs. Most have had the original engines replaced with Toyota and Mitsubishi diesels.

On the first day, we went to the Partagas Cigar Factory and took a three-hour convertible tour of the city ('55 pink Ford, '57 purple Ford, and '57 pink Pontiac). We visited a park and saw the remains of Gary Powers' U2 that was shot down. (That shooting was over Russia, but Rudolf Anderson was shot down over Cuba in 1962.) We also partied at the Buena Vista Social Club. I think I saw Desi Arnaz and Lucy in the audience (maybe it was the rum).

The second day was "Art Day" – museums, visiting artists' houses, etc.

On the third day, we traveled to Trinidad, 300-plus kilometers in three classic taxis. Envision 75-80 MPH – no seat belts – no air bags – no mufflers – no worries. P.S. The driver was periodically texting and playing music videos on a dashboard screen. Life in the fast lane! Kinda like running with scissors.

We also encountered tens of thousands of land crabs in the road over a stretch of 5-6 miles. They apparently were migrating for mating season. So now you have the answer to the age-old question, "Why did the land crab cross the road?" It is "To have sex!"

We spent a day in Trinidad on a walking tour and a visit to a slave plantation (where sugarcane was raised), and the next day we returned to Havana by old train and auto, followed by dinner and the ballet.

The sixth day was Hemingway Day with a visit to his casa. We saw his boat, which was the basis for *The Old Man and the Sea*. The guard suggested that I should charge for pics with it due to my "Hemingway mustache." We went to the town where the real Old Man, Santiago, lived and fished, and had daiquiris at the bar Papa frequented. Then we went back to Havana and had daiquiris at the Floridita Bar where Papa also imbibed. Maybe I'll be a writer when I grow up? Saturday evening was dinner and a show at the Tropicana Club – lots of showgirls, but who noticed?

After getting to the hotel about 12:30 AM, we got up at 4:30 AM to go to the airport. Party animals all around?

Overall, the trip was an experience. Contrary to popular belief, the food was excellent. We didn't drink the water and thus had no *disenteria* (Spanish for "trots"). The people were warm and friendly. However, the infrastructure is in terrible shape. Most of the newer buildings are Soviet Architorture (boxes), and in general, all maintenance has been abandoned since the Soviets pulled out in the 1990s. Our bottom line is that Cuba is definitely worth a trip to see for yourself. We are glad we went, but we wouldn't go back for a second trip.

P.S. After eight days, I couldn't get the song "Guantanamera" out of my head! Luckily, I found it on Pandora.

The 50th Anniversary Tour

As a part of celebrating 50 WONDERFUL years together we toured Spain and Portugal in March-April 2017.

First let me set the stage – a doddering, elderly couple was celebrating their 50th wedding anniversary in Spain and Portugal. Their first stop was Barcelona. Since they had never been there before, they set up a three-hour tour of the city. Wait!!! – Here it comes – ON A MOTOR-CYCLE WITH A SIDECAR! Are they Damned Old Fools or adventurous seniors? You decide.

Our motorcycle guide, an Italian named Giorgio, was an aspiring musician looking for that big break in "the Musical Biz." However, in the reality time before the Grammys, he puts food on the table by being a motorcycle tour driver.

The bikes they use are Russian Euros (which are knock-offs of the BMW WWII sidecar motorcycles – obviously stolen from BMW by Russian hackers).

So we put on helmets equipped with microphones and headphones and mounted up, the Queen in the royal sidecar and me hanging my butt off in back of the driver. The Ruskies don't do soft seats.

Spanish drivers are like Italian drivers (Giorgio fit in here) and Florida drivers. Road rules include:

1. Speed limits are interpretable guidelines.

2. We don't need any stinking turn signals.

3. Horns rule.

Oh, and about 50% of the vehicles on the road are motor scooters.

The Queen looked mega-royal doing her Queenie wave to the crowding loyal followers on the streets.

Fun evening. We survived with no hospital visits. The only "injury" was that the Queen got "helmet hair," which had to be medicated with vodka. Dr. Mike to the rescue.

On the second day, we did a tour of Barcelona with a driver and guide, a more "Queenly" approach to touristing. The highlight of the tour was the cathedral "Sagrada Familia" (Sacred Family) by Gaudi, Spain's most famous architect. It has been under construction since 1883 and is about 3/4 completed. I haven't seen anything like it. If you google "Sagrada Familia," you will see what I mean. Then we did a tapas (small plate) walking tour, and three of us shared ten tapas (muy bueno) plus rioja (red) wine.

On the third day, "WE" took a Spanish cooking class. Right up there on MY bucket list for sure! We started at the Barcelona market and purchased everything needed to make a fish and meat paella. Then we went to the cooking school and spent three hours preparing the meal. Everyone had specific jobs to do. My jobs were (1) wine taster, (2) picture taker, and (3) nap leader for the siesta following the meal. And I am proud to report that I aced all three! I am not surprised that the Queen declared her paella better than the cooking school chef's – are you?

On the fourth day, we got up early and caught a high-speed train to Madrid. We went on an auto tour of the city, saw the bull-fighting arena, visited an artist who makes guitars, and watched a hand-crafted bookbinder. Yawn! TGFR (Thank God for Rioja!)

After the cooking school, the guitar maker and the

bookbinder blew my Culture-O-Meter off the charts. I wondered if my heart could take more La Vida En El Carril Rapido (life in the fast lane). Hang on – the intensity builds!

On the fifth day, we started in Madrid at the Royal Palace where the King of Spain allegedly lives (but doesn't – he lives outside the city). THREE HOURS of studying royal tapestries, royal china, royal clocks, and royal silverware. Nothing like jumpstarting your morning! Next we visited the royal tapestry factory to watch tapestry being made and repaired. Yes, it's like watching paint dry! However, the real highlight (seriously) was the Museo del Prado (Prado Museum), which is the Spanish National Art Museum. It has over 8,600 paintings and 700 sculptures by the major European masters. Fifty years after taking Art History 101 at PSU, I was able to use it!

On Day 6, we caught a high-speed train to Córdoba and toured the city. From there, we took a car to Seville. I probably shouldn't bring the next incident up because, if it gets out, I'll never be allowed back in Texas: the Queen and I took a Flamenco lesson. At first, I thought she said, "Flamingo" and wondered why anyone would imitate a plastic lawn ornament. Since she was persistent (OK, more like threatening our 50 years of blissful marriage with a costly divorce), I eventually condescended (caved). We took a one-hour private lesson with the lead dancer at the Museo del Baile Flamenco. We found that the Flamenco is much more difficult than the Twist or the Electric Slide – in addition to moving your feet, you do a lot of hand gestures, clapping, and stomping – more like a Spanish polka? After the lesson, we attended a Flamenco show at the Museo where our instructor and her husband starred. Kinda cool, sitting in the audience and telling everyone, "Yes, she's the one who taught me."

After the show, the Queen went shopping for traje de flamenca (a dress, shawl, and heeled dancing shoes), and this morning she had her hair in a bun. Me? I'm trying to find toreador pants.

Then we toured Bodega Lustau in the heart of sherry country. For those who may not be familiar with sherry, it is "fortified" wine – they add alcohol (novel idea) – and it is NOT the dessert wines usually seen being sipped by the little old ladies (Q Tips) in Geezerville. I'll describe the tour for you up to the point that my memory gets hazy (about the eleventh of eighteen different sherry products). Lustau is a boutique manufacturer selling about 400,000 bottles a year, and their storage/aging area has 12,000 casks. The tour included delicious tapas of cheeses, meats, olives, etc. Next thing – we were back in Seville. I believe this is called "a mobile siesta." Not to worry – we had a non-tasting driver.

The next stop was a Seville PCP tour (Palaces, Cathedrals, and Parks).

We spent the second week in Portugal, first in the capital, Lisbon, then in the second-largest city, Porto.

Okay, let's be honest. As Dr. Phil would note, Portugal has a Napoleon Complex when it comes to Spain. They come up short – one-fifth the population, one-sixth the size, and one-sixth the GNP. And it irritates them (euphemism for "pisses them off"). Size matters. They point out that Portugal had one of the largest and longest colonial empires between 1400 and 2000. Their explorers sailed the world and claimed all kinds of places. True.

True. True. What they don't mention is that they couldn't defend these lands from larger countries and lost them. Size matters!

We drove to Sintra to see the summer residences (palaces) of the kings. We also went to the westernmost point of continental Europe and took the obligatory "Japanese Tourist" pictures. (No, we didn't use a selfie stick, so we weren't true JT's.)

Then we drove to Porto, home of port wine, and did a tasting tour of the Churchill winery and a river tour.

Next, we toured the Douro River valley and the Sandeman winery. Our hostess was dressed in the Sandeman black cape and sombrero, and with her ruby-red makeup, nose ring, and tongue stud, she looked like Lady Dracula. I kept my cross ready.

Speaking of crosses, there are 75 cathedrals in Porto – so many churches to see, so little time! On the other hand, there are 82 port wineries in Porto – so many ports to taste, so little time!!!

And finally, we started our journey home at 4 AM. Of course, we had the typical delays, lost luggage, etc., but it's what we love about travel.

P.S. The royal luggage arrived in Geezerville a day later.

When asked "How did you like your trip?" I use words like educational, developmental, and memorable. That way no one knows, it sounds thoughtful, and I can focus on spring trout fishing in PA.

2018 Travel

Due to a series of injuries including falling off a ladder and fracturing four ribs and pinching nerves in the back while exercising and golfing, we had no major travel in 2018 except for the trips between Geezerville and the fish camp and frequent visits to our doctors and therapists.

From Russia with Love Tour

Even though we purchased a new house in January 2019, moved in February, and sold our condo in April, we didn't slow down when it came to travel. This was primarily due to our having booked two trips prior to these events. In May 2019, the Queen and I joined three friends (Carrie, Tam, and Charlene) for a trip to Russia – four days in St. Petersburg, then six days on the *Volga Dream* river cruise ship, and four days in Moscow. The royal entourage (one Queen, one scribe/treasurer/gofer (Mikhaïl), and three ladies-in-waiting – Charlene, Carrie, and Tam) left the States for St. Petersburg, Russia. We all arrived safely, after 20 hours, with one exception – the Keebaugh luggage caravan. It was either in Paris or Amsterdam or _____ (fill in a city of your choice). Delta and Air France were subjected to the Queen's Royal Wrath, and the rest of our party was strafed by friendly fire as the Queen told everyone in the city. Thirty hours late, the luggage arrived.

To show how well we absorbed the museum, architecture, and arts material we saw and heard about, I have added a Culture Meter (Culture-O-Meter) reading at the end of each day.

Arrival: Culture-O-Meter reading –– Low –– Beverly Hillbillies level.

On the first day in St. Petersburg, we had a private tour – caviar/champagne tasting (seven types – outstanding!), Sts. Peter and Paul's Cathedral (where the royals are buried) and the Grand Choral Synagogue (second largest in Europe).

Culture-O-Meter reading –– Safe –– The caviar and champagne lowered the cathedral overload.

One new twist to visiting public displays in Russia is the Nyet Nyet ladies. They wear black clothes, sit in a corner, and if you get too close to an exhibit, they come flying at you screaming, "NYET, NYET!!"

On the second day, we toured St. Isaac's Cathedral and the Catherine Palace.

Culture-O-Meter reading –– Warning!! –– Stop all museum activity and lubricate brain with Vodka.

On the third day we toured the Winter Palace, the Hermitage Museum, the Gold Room, and the Peterhof (summer palace).

Culture-O-Meter reading –– Danger!! –– Pretentious material build-up in brain. May start speaking French.

On the fourth day we toured the Faberge museum and the Amber Room.

Culture-O-Meter reading –– May Day! May Day! –– Further absorption impossible! CULTURE COMA.

The tour company hooked us up with three others, an Australian (James) and a Canadian couple (Genevieve and Bill). In the spirit of international cooperation, we accepted them into the group on a probationary basis; however, Bill had already gotten me in trouble with the Nyet Nyet ladies in a monastery and was in danger of being kicked off the island at any time.

The river cruise ship is called the *Volga Dream* (VD). Is it named for the river we were on? Nyet and even Nyet! Nyet! Of the 850 miles on the cruise, only one-tenth was on the Volga. The rest was on the Neva River, Lake Ladoga, the Svir River, the Lower Sheksna River, Rybinsk Reservoir, and the Moscow Canal (including seven locks – zero bagels – quit groaning – I know it was bad).

The VD accommodated 105 passengers and was well done, including FOOD. We adopted a server, Ludmila (Luda), who was outstanding. I think the Queen invited her to Florida or added her to the will or something. Did I mention the volume and quality of FOOD available?

As reported above, I was in a cultural coma – too many cathedrals, castles, and museums over the four days in St. Petersburg. I was confusing Peter the Great with Ivan the Terrible, with all 47 of the Nicholases, and with Andrée the Only.

By the way, if I was a czar, I'd choose the superlative. Why be "Michael the Great" when you could be "Michael the Greatest"?

Fortunately, the first day of the river cruise was in Svirstroy, a large hydroelectric station and a concentration camp. (Yes, the two are connected – guess who built the station?) We visited a local family (Grandma looked like Aunt Bea on the *Andy Griffith Show*) and a musical school. The Culture intensity level fell dramatically.

The second day we visited Kizhi Island to see how the settlers lived 500 years ago in a harsh environment – minus 40 (C and F both – check it out). Our guide said, "In the winter we wear our fur coats buttoned. In the summer we wear our fur coats unbuttoned."

The Culture-O-Meter reading was still going down.

This was the day of the Giant Mosquito Attack. They carried off the small children and gnawed at the rest of us.

The third day we visited Goritsy and had a TWO-HOUR monastery tour Which Should Have Lasted TEN MINUTES. The Culture-O-Meter exploded. I could only imagine the movie *Groundhog Day* – waking up the next morning and hearing the guide drone on. Thankfully, this was followed by a Russian dinner and vodka tasting to lower the tension. Did I mention the volume and quality of FOOD available?

The fourth day was Yaroslavl and a city tour. Beautiful tour and Beautiful Guide.

The fifth day was Uglich and another cathedral tour. I am a survivor.

We spent the final four days of our trip in Moscow. Moscow is kinda like NYC, DC, and LA all rolled into one – mega-city, government center, and entertainment producer. With a population of 13 million (not to be confused with Moscow, PA, population 2,000), it's the northernmost and coldest mega-city in the world – however, it was in the 80s F when we were there. Al Gore predicted this.

We stayed in the Four Seasons Hotel next to the Kremlin and Red Square.

Right in the center of all the action. Literally. While we were in Russia, Ivan Golunov, an investigative reporter, was falsely arrested on fabricated drug charges and finally released. As a result, there was a demonstration to protest "police fabrication." Right in our neighborhood, Mr. Rogers! Over 400 were detained. There were police stationed every ten feet. We used the chameleon strategy – stay low and get the HELL outta Dodge.

Prior to the unscheduled activities, we toured the Kremlin (seat of government), the Armory Museum, the Metro (high-speed, clean, and decorated with sculptures), the old Tretyakov Gallery, Tolstoy's House (Mr. *War and Peace*), and Cafe Zhivago (where I was mistaken for Omar Sharif – NYET!).

By the way – at the Armory Chamber of the Kremlin Museum we found out that when royals traveled, they had to take their throne with them to make their eminence known. Guess I need to add four royal throne bearers to the Queen's entourage for the next trip?

We also visited Bunker-42, a hidden underground strategic (nuclear) air force command and control center (recently declassified). The nuclear-blast-protected facility is 700 feet deep or eighteen stories of steep steps, and we climbed every one of them – eat your heart out, you Stairmaster weenies. (OK – full disclosure is: we did the stairs going down and rode an elevator going back up – but we would have done them if one of the team didn't have a bad knee – so there!!!)

Our final tour was the Gulag Museum which was depressing, thinking that 18 million people were sentenced to be "cleansed." (The state made use of this workforce and created an economic entity.) Our guide was from Siberia, and he claimed his grandfather was sentenced because while he was hanging a picture of Stalin, he hit his finger and swore at the picture – ??? By the way, this is the same Joseph Stalin who was quoted as saying, "Gaiety is among the most outstanding features of the Soviet Union."

One final observation – the police and the limo drivers continually played cat-and-mouse games. For example: 1. Our driver was about to get a ticket for illegal parking. All of the sudden, the two of them went to the back of the vehicle and the driver paid off the cop. (The system works – money talks.) 2. You must pay to park and the police use an automated system to drive around and scan/record license plates for later matching against payers and freeloaders. Our driver put on a phony magnetic plate (the Invisible Van? – OK. I got my bad pun in). 3. Our driver had a bogus "Handicapped" hang tag, claiming his grandmother needed it. (The Queen was designated Grandmother of the Day.)

In summary for the trip:

1. Overall a lot of fun and interesting.

2. Great group to travel with.

3. Excellent food.

4. Need to have a "speed tour" guide, kinda like speed dating. Focus on highlights. I'm not earning a PhD in 16th-century buttons.

5. Russian democracy is only 27 years old. It will take time to evolve.

6. The Queen liked it, so we all liked it!

The group we were with made the trip – from the ladies-in-waiting (Charlene, Carrie, and Tam) to our adopted new friends (James, Genevieve, and Bill). Thanks to all of you.

TSA Foils Mustache Bomber

I don't know whether it hit your local papers or not, but in June 2019, the TSA took down a major terror plot right here in State College, PA, USA, and the Queen and I were there to witness it!

It all started when we were flying from SC to Philadelphia on the first leg of our World Polka Tour. No, I didn't say "World Poker Tour." It's a tour of the Czech Republic, where the Polka was born, and a river cruise between Bucharest and Budapest, a Bohemian area where Lawrence Welk rules. But I digress.

The Queen and I checked the royal luggage, and each took a carry-on bag to the security line. Andrée sailed through, and I went through the machine okay, but when my bag hit the scanner, the diligent tech noticed two suspicious-looking containers. After a second run, she elevated the issue to her supervisor, Ms. Personality. She rummaged through my bag and extracted two containers filled with "white powder." She ran it through the sniffer, and all hell broke loose. Red lights flashed, alarms sounded, and I was shuffled off to the contamination area. (I am not making this up.) While I was undressed and body-searched, Ms. I'm-In-Charge called her supervisor, who was probably in a covert bunker in Montana, for guidance. They decided to have Andrée put the containers in our checked luggage while I remained under "house arrest." When she returned, I was freed.

So by now you have to be asking: what was in the containers????

It was MIRALAX, the powder to relieve occasional irregularity. I shit you not! (So to speak!) Apparently, there are videos on the net describing how to make a bomb from MIRALAX??? What's next – toilet paper????

When I became a free man again, the first thing I did was to go have a couple beers since the plane we were to take was called back to the gate twice for mechanical problems, and this meant we couldn't make the flight from Philadelphia to London. FIVE HOURS MORE IN THE SCE AIRPORT!!!! Is this a good start or what???

The B2B Tour (Bucharest to Budapest)

After escaping the TSA crackdown smackdown in State College and arriving in Prague (amazingly only five hours later than planned) – with our combustible MIRALAX safely contained! We were back on Plan A – spend a couple days in Prague on our own, then join up with our friends Shari and Rod Erlich on a river cruise of the Danube – B2B or Bucharest To Budapest.

Prague is a beautiful city and the most cheerful of those we visited. The first day we did a walking tour of the city, and the second day we toured the Jewish section of Prague, including the cemetery where 100,000 are buried in 8,000 or so graves (Think – bunk beds).

On the third day we traveled on Czech Air (which makes Southwest look like first class) to Bucharest, Romania, motto "Home of Dracula, the Securitate Police State, and other fun things." We met the Erlichs, but not their luggage. It went MIA (Missing in Airport) between Heathrow and Budapest. Shari purchased replacement clothing. Rod was able to shop for temporary clothes, but Romania's finest made him look like Dan Ackroyd and

Steve Martin in a SNL "Wild and Crazy Guys" skit. This was MIA Day 1.

We also discovered MGen Craig Cooper (Ret), his wife Susan, and his Air Force friend Pete Forman and his wife Debi on board. Craig was an Air Force acquisition officer before he retired and became the president of a defense company's business segment, and we had worked together on a number of developments. And finally, we met a great couple from Charleston, SC, Jack and Susan Dawson. The five couples became "Insta-Friends" and spent a lot of time together doing what you do on cruises (eat, drink, and visit cathedrals/museums/monuments – did I mention eat and drink?). We became the cruise director's Problem Children, requesting special accommodations like a table for ten, special wine, etc. The Queen even went so far as to have them write her name on the bottles of a Pinot Noir she liked. This ain't hyperbole, it's true!!

On Saturday we embarked on the *MS Esprit*, our home for the next week. There were 67 of us and 41 crew, so we were treated well. We visited the mountains of Romania on Saturday and the Black Sea at Constanta on Sunday.

P.S. Saturday was MIA Day 2. Here's a little-known fact. Romanian underwear has no fly, and the pants have buttons, not zippers. So one needs to plan rest stops with sufficient lead time, or he will end up doing the dinky dance.

Sunday was MIA Day 3. At this point, Rod resorted to the old college technique of turning one's underwear inside out to get an extra day of wear. Rod also contacted the British Airways call center, but Raj had never heard of Heathrow.

On Monday, MIA Day 4, we visited Ruse, Bulgaria and on Tuesday, MIA Day 5, it was Vidin, Bulgaria, both so absolutely stunning that I don't remember anything about them. Apparently our tour company, Tauck, doesn't either since I couldn't find it in their literature.

Great news on MIA Day 4 – Shari's luggage arrived! Also, Rod's was found in Ghana, Africa. Understandable mistake since Bucharest's airport code is OTP and Ghana's code is ACC. Easy to confuse!!!! Rod celebrated by going commando.

On Day 5 we all showed our support to Rod by going commando!!! Rod's luggage arrived in the afternoon.

The moral to the story is – don't get overly excited about things that happen to you – take things as they come – relax and enjoy life. Hey, this makes a good Life Lesson.

Life Lesson 76: Don't Get Your Shorts in A Knot – EVEN IF YOU DON'T HAVE SHORTS!!!!

Scribe's Note: Thanks to my friend Rod for letting me embellish the underwear story. To my knowledge, no underwear was inverted, and no one went commando. But then again, who knows?

This was an interesting trip to this point. Our intrepid team has survived the MIRALAX threat and the luggage excursion (by the way, Rod's bags earned 4,290 frequent flyer miles for the trip to Ghana), and we managed to tour the Czech Republic, Romania, and Bulgaria even with these diversions.

So let's just pick up on Day 6 with a trip through the Iron Gates, the set of locks that made navigation on the Danube possible, a double lock that raised us 100 feet. This "damn dam" essentially flooded many of the towns, and they had to be relocated. But "C'est la vie," which means "tough noogies" in French.

I was impressed that given all the hardships, the local people have not lost their sense of humor. For example, at dinner one evening when I was offered soup, I said, "No, thanks, mustaches and soup don't go together," and the young waitress immediately said, "My grandmother says the same thing." Knocked me off my chair!

Then Day 7 was Belgrade, Serbia, which was part of the former Yugoslavia and ruled for many years by Tito. Ah, they don't make dictators like that anymore. We had dinner in the palace, hosted by the crown prince and his wife. Unfortunately, nobody has told this guy that the monarchy is long gone, won't be returning, and he will never ever get crowned. So he needs to get a life.

Time for a factoid – Belgrade is the city with the largest number of Serbs in the world. What is number two? ————-(no peeking)

Answer – Chicago! – Surprise! Surprise! Surprise!

Day 8 was Croatia to see the after-effects of the Serbian-Croatian War bombing and to visit with a couple who lived through it. Very moving and sad.

Friday was also the ship dance contest, which was won by our very own Dancing Queen and one of the ship's waiters dressed as Elvis. Unfortunately, I am not making this up!! I have pictures!

Then we visited Hungary, including wine tasting in Villany and several days in Budapest (lovely city).

The countries we visited have several things in common: They were repeatedly attacked over the ages, gaining and losing territory; they chose the losing side in the World Wars; they were dominated by the Soviet Union for long periods of history (and many buildings suffer from Soviet "Architorture"); and they are struggling with being poor and trying to become democracies.

My advice to them is if your country's name ends in "ia" (Romania, Bulgaria, Serbia, Croatia, etc.), change it! Also, get some zippers for your pants and put flies in your tighty-whiteys.

Now for the *coup de grace*. We got up at 3 AM Wednesday (this was 9 PM EDT Tuesday) to fly home. All was A-OK, hunky-dory, copacetic until we landed in Philadelphia, where our flight to State College was cancelled. After six hours of flight changes, additional cancelations, and plodding from gate to gate, we landed in State College at 12:30 AM Thursday (27-plus hours later) WITHOUT OUR LUGGAGE!!!

P.S. Best of all – the Queen's dancing trophy arrived unharmed.

P.S.S. I have sworn off airline travel forever.

P.S.S.S. (If there is such a thing) I think Elvis is moving in with us, and he and the Queen are auditioning for *Dancing with The Stars*?

Now let's move on to PART IV, which is OBSERVATIONS, a compilation of things I have seen and noted over the years.

PART IV: OBSERVATIONS

The next six chapters cover a potpourri of things I have observed and conclusions I have drawn over the years. OK, I just gave you another $10 word, potpourri, which is French for "a lot of stuff poured from a pot." All of this is gratis, which is also a free word (that's a two-fer in one paragraph) meaning "at no extra charge." So this "free stuff poured from a pot" includes chapters on Change, Inventions, Politics, and the Universal People Segmentation Rule (the 5/95 Rule).

Chapter 21:
Change

Life Lesson 77: Life is like underwear: change is good.

I have lived in a period of unprecedented change, and even today the pace of change continues to accelerate. Let me give you some examples.

Television

I grew up with three network channels and lots of snow on a mini screen in a box that weighed more than I did. Today, Comcast Xfinity advertises over 260 channels. And you still can't find anything good to view, so most viewers stick with a handful of channels that they regularly watch.

Speaking of Xfinity, and cable in general, we didn't have any of that back in the stone ages, sonny. We had antennas. The people in cities had "rabbit ears," a pair of 15" antennas in a V shape that sat on the TV. We folks out in the small towns needed much more. My father, an ex-airplane mechanic, built a 60-foot triangular tower that was hinged to a concrete base and secured with airplane cable-guy wires. We were the talk of the town in McConnellsburg, PA.

Perhaps the biggest addition to the television lineup

over the years has been the 24-hour news channels, complete with scrolling headlines and talking heads. They mostly show two people arguing vehemently with each other for hours on end. You can find stations that support any political view, and you can tell a lot about people if you know what channels they watch.

For example, CNN is oriented toward the liberals, Fox News rallies the conservatives, and MSNBC doesn't have a clue.

With 24-hour news, the world never sleeps. If an event occurs, it is broadcast and known worldwide in minutes. This often leads to reactions that haven't been fully thought out, including "Twitter Storms."

And what about weather reporting? I remember the local weatherman getting a three-minute slot on the news to give tomorrow's forecast. Who ever dreamed that one would spend hours on end watching the Weather Channel? Well, just wait until a hurricane begins to form offshore. The reporters drone on for hours about the latest forecast of intensity and predicted path. This leads us to Life Lesson 78.

Life Lesson 78: If Jim Cantore shows up in your town, get the hell out!

You don't want to see the Weather Channel's man on the scene hanging horizontally on a street sign, dressed in logo rain gear, telling you how bad it's going to become.

I have already discussed the Food Network channel and HDTV, and there are many other "specialty channels" available such as shopping networks, pet networks (for your poodle), National Geographic networks (armchair adventure), Disney networks (aka "babysitters"), travel networks (see the world from your La-Z-Boy), PBS networks (watch people in a studio taking pledges for a telethon), local government networks (if you're really hard up for something to watch), etc. You can watch sports (some may be totally new to you like extreme shuffleboard, hog-calling, and tractor pulls), ethnic channels of all flavors and languages, and comedy and movies out the gazoo. You can also listen to music of your choice.

The acceptable mores for words and topics permitted on TV have expanded greatly over time (mostly downhill) to reflect our culture. For example, TV has made erectile dysfunction (ED) a household term because of widespread advertising of Viagra and Cialis. But hold on there. We guys now have a new malady to worry about, and the drug companies are doing their civic duty in informing the public. It is called Peyronie's Disease, which is a bent erect penis. Have you seen the ads yet? They start with men holding up raw vegetables, most impressively a foot-long cucumber, and the tag line "men come in all shapes and sizes." If only I was making up this stiff – sorry, typo – should be "stuff." Apparently, there are two remedies for Peyronie's, traction therapy and XIAFLEX. I know where my vote would be!

Television technology

From the days of three channels and snowy screens, today we have high-definition digital TVs, flat screens, pictures that measure up to hundreds of inches, digital recording, voice recognition, 4K pixels, sound bars, and wireless speakers. Never mind that we can't afford furniture for the house, we gotta have these gadgets!

Another new feature is streaming channels on the internet. You can watch anything at any time and anywhere on any device. You can see any movie ever made. Where do we go from here? If you didn't need food and toilet paper, you would never have to leave the house. Wait a minute – you can order these online, Mr. Hermit.

And the cost of this cable TV is ONLY hundreds of dollars per month.

By the way, the cable purveyors are notorious for offering a cut-rate price to get your business and then gouging you after the initial period. This means that once a year, you must call them and say, "I found a much better deal with your competitor, Superdupervision." They will cave and give you a reduced "loyalty package" price to stay. Oh, the games we play.

YouTube

This leads me to YouTube. If you want to do something, Mr. Fix-it, you can find multiple how-to videos that walk you through the exercise step by step. User manuals are extinct. I use YouTube to learn how to operate new features on my computer and to do almost any installation task. Need to know how to replace a battery in a 2014 BMW 640i's key fob? There is a YouTube video that walks you through it.

You can also find videos of dumbasses attempting stupid tricks which almost always result in a catastrophe. These clips usually start with "Hey! Hold my beer and watch this." Remember Life Lesson 79.

Life Lesson 79: If you play with fire, video it for YouTube.

Facebook

Here we see people sharing their lives with their friends. Many times these are things that shouldn't be shared. We show pictures and videos of our travels. This is an invitation to burglars that says, "Hey, I'm going to be away for the next fourteen days. Rob me blind, sucker." The only thing we don't reveal is that the key is under the mat. We see pictures from restaurants of our "friends'" meals. Do you really care what your friends are eating? I don't know about you, but my Give-A-Damn's busted. On the positive side, we can wish each other Happy Birthday without buying a four-dollar card and a seven-dollar stamp. We also see political extremism. And we share all this with our "friends."

Smart appliances

Everything you buy today is "smart," i.e., it contains a computer. Examples are appliances, automobiles, and phones. And we have everything connected via Wi-Fi. I can adjust my house thermostat, control my garage door, and see who's at my front door from Timbuktu if I ever have a reason to be there. I particularly like my garage door opener. How many times have you driven away and thought, "Did I close the garage door?" I have an app (does that sound techy or what?) that tells me if it is open or closed and lets me close it if necessary. Peace of mind.

The app also permits me to order from Amazon specifying "garage delivery," which gives the Amazon driver the capability to open my garage door and leave packages inside and not on the porch. Is that cool or what? By the way, I used YouTube to help me set it all up.

On the downside, the technology is often beyond our ability to use it. This is captured in Life Lesson 80.

Life Lesson 80: Don't buy anything that is smarter than you are.

You won't be able to set it up, use it, or pay for it. And Artificial Intelligence means the device will continue to get smarter. George Orwell's *1984* has arrived. Conspiracy Alert! Our smart devices are watching us, tracking what we do, and reporting back to _____.
Please fill in the blank with the name of your favorite:

1. Three letter domestic intelligence agency (CIA, NSA, DNI, NRO, etc.)

2. Foreign intelligence agency (M5, M6, KGB – oh yeah, the KGB went away, didn't they? Right-o, Vladimir!)

3. Country (pick a country, any country)

4. Tech company (Apple, Google – my tech assistant, Mr. Google denies it – Facebook, etc.)

5. Neighbor

6. Automobile

7. Or simply write in "All of the Above"

Think you are alone and invisible? FUGGEDABOU-TIT!

User-friendly

Today everything is user-friendly. No one wants to buy a user-hostile product. But user-friendly is an oxymoron. As Dave Barry has noted, "The word 'user' is used by the computer professionals when they mean 'idiot'." User-friendly really means if you have an IQ of 150 or above, and you have an advanced degree in the computer sciences, you might figure it out in a month or so. Otherwise, call the help desk.

Speaking of help desks, all tech companies have one. It is a bank of "agent experts" of unknown nationality, in an unknown location, speaking Semi-English, that you can call for technical assistance. After waiting in line from 30 minutes to two days (the world record held by Homer Bigbottom from Newark, NJ), listening to the message that you hear over and over – "All of our agents are currently assisting other customers. Please stay on the line. We will be with you shortly" – you finally connect with Raj, who says "How may I assist your problem?" Raj then asks you for all of your profile data, including the name of your first-grade teacher, your weight and height, your arrest record, etc. These are things that are needed to "assist your problem." Then Raj says, "Permit me one moment to investigate." After five minutes or so, Raj comes back on the line and informs you that your issue is really best handled by another department and he will transfer you. The line goes dead. Meanwhile, the seven-year-old neighbor kid stops by and in 30 seconds has you up and running.

An offspring of the help desk is the live chat, where you communicate with an automated agent in an inter-active session. The new twist here is that the system first uses Artificial Intelligence in an automated Q&A with you to "assist your problem." This is done to avoid waking Raj and his backroom cronies to help. Sounds cool, but I haven't seen any successes yet. Wake up, Raj. You're on, Mr. Guru.

Bottled Water and Starbucks

Who woulda thunk that today we would pay exorbitant prices for water in a plastic bottle and Hooty Tooty cof-fee? Well, my friend, remember it's 1984.

Inventions

As an engineer, I am fascinated with inventions that have impacted mankind (and womankind). So let me start off by talking about them – the good, the bad, and the ugly. I've developed my own top ten lists of the best inventions ever, the worst inventions ever, and the buggy whips cre-ated by inventions.

Chapter 22:
Top 10 Best Inventions

1. Toilet paper – Surprise? Well, it shouldn't be. Just think how the progress of mankind would have been slowed by sore and itchy bottoms. Our ancestors had to use leaves, grass, ferns, corncobs, fruit skins, seashells, sand, stones, moss, snow and water. Of course, the simple solution was to wipe with your hand. This gives rise to a twist on the age-old parable, "Don't bite the hand that feeds you," which becomes Life Lesson 81.

> ## Life Lesson 81: Don't wipe the hand that feeds you.

Of course, our wealthy ancestors used wool, lace, and hemp.

Joseph "Charmin Joe" Gayetty is widely credited with being the inventor of commercially available toilet paper. He introduced it in 1857, and the original advertisements for this product used the tagline "The greatest necessity of the age! Gayetty's medicated paper for the water closet." On behalf of mankind everywhere, thank you, Charmin Joe.

2. Computers and Communication Devices – Ok, call me Mr. Cop-Out, but I have lumped a myriad of modern computing and communication equipment together. If

I listed each one as an invention, we would have nothing else on the list. Give me a break, Mr. Nerd or Ms. Nerdette. Computers and communications have changed our whole lifestyle. I am particularly fond of computers because they enabled my career. I have a BA in Math, where I was introduced to Computer Science, and a MS in Computer Science. The first part of my career was in software development. My timing was fortuitous. I started in intelligence and signal processing just as the industry was moving from special-purpose hardware to incorporating computers and software solutions. We programmed in assembly language (pseudo machine code), we developed our own operating systems, and we did real-time signal processing – all on computers with less power than my Apple Watch. What a trip!

For computers, I include the ENIAC (the first commercial digital computer, weighing in at 30 tons and containing 18,000 vacuum tubes), "the big iron" from IBM, which today stands for I've Been Mothballed (by Apple and other startups), supercomputers, PCs, laptops, iPads, smart watches, Fitbits, smart phones, etc.

For communications devices, I include mobile phones and car phones (remember the "shoeboxes" we mounted on the floorboards and the spiral antennas on the car window or roof?), cell phones, smart phones, smart watches, Wi-Fi, 1G through 5G mobile comms technology (G as in Generation, not G-String, you slackers), etc.

On behalf of mankind everywhere, thank you, Al Gore, for inventing computers and the internet.

3. Super glue – Super glue is an amazing invention. You can stick anything you want together. Super glue it and

it's a permanent bond. You can also stick things you don't want to put together like your fingers, the object you are gluing and the dining room table, your dog and the carpet, and my wife's favorite unmentioned body extremity should I ever cheat on her. This brings to mind Life Lesson 82.

Life Lesson 82: What super glue has brought together, let no man put asunder.

4. Football – Isn't it great that we can spend our Sundays, Monday nights, and Thursday nights watching pro football, all day Saturday watching college football, and don't forget Friday-night high school football. And when the NFL, college and high school seasons end, the hardcore football junkie can watch arena football (April through August) and the Canadian Football League (June through October). Is life good or what? Of course, I'm talking about real American football, and not that shorty-shorts European knock-off version. Football has become America's most popular sport, displacing baseball with its seemingly endless game duration, and lawn bowling. (Not! I only added lawn bowling to check the reader's attention level.) Imagine, without football we wouldn't have a Super Bowl with its two-hour half-time Broadway extravaganza and those ridiculously priced, great commercial ads – the real reason most people watch.

Why is football so popular in America? Commentator George Will gives us Life Lesson 83.

Life Lesson 83: Football combines two bad features of American life – it is violence punctuated by committee meetings.

And here I thought it was the Dallas Cowboys Cheer-leaders?

Football has created a raison d'etre (French for money source) for WSJ columnist Jason Gay, who writes about the personality quirks of the Patriots' coach, the Grumpy Old Lobster Boat Captain, Bill Belichick. Way to exploit it, Wall Street Jay.

5. Fast food – Remember in the olden days before McDonald's? Prehistoric, right? McDonald's has introduced a whole new cuisine and language, McSpeak, to the world, e.g., McNuggets, Supersize, McRib, Big Mac, Egg McMuffin, etc. McDonald's has also created a new career path for Liberal Arts graduates. (Practice this line, you Theater Arts majors: "You want fries with that?") McDonald's led the way, and others followed with a plethora of food choices.

Hey – plethora (abundance) is another word worth the price of this book. By the time you finish reading it, you will be orating with eloquence and panache.

6. Mr. Google, the world's fastest researcher and smartest person – What did we do before Google? In the "good old days," we used dictionaries and encyclopedias. Boring! Google tells it like it is and Now. If Mr. Google ever got on *Jeopardy*, look out, Jeopardy James, the mega-winner.

Your record would be in jeopardy, so to speak. Mr. Google's answers would come so fast that Alex Trebek would be doing a song and dance to fill time.

Mr. Google's birth name was Googol, the number one followed by 100 zeros, which signified that he could handle large quantities of data. For privacy reasons, he changed it to Google when he started using online dating services.

7. Indoor plumbing – Did you ever experience having to go while on a camping trip in the middle of January and then tramping through the snow at two AM to an outhouse to do your business? If not, I don't wish it upon you. You freeze your tooties and everything else. According to the website portapotty.net (I am not making this up. Check it out, you nonbelievers), the history of indoor plumbing goes back to 6000 BC.

Contrary to popular belief, Thomas Crapper did not invent the toilet in the 18th century, although he did own an English plumbing company. Sorry, Tommy, Al Gore invented it – just messing with you. Legend has it that King Minos of Crete invented it around 4000 BC.

Another fun fact for you – the average person spends three years of his life on the can. Perhaps you are reading this from the throne? Perhaps you should be?

8. The microwave oven – Actually this was invented by some engineers at Raytheon by mistake. They found microwaves melted the candy bars in their shirt pockets. I hope they had the chocolate bars in their pocket protectors. Of course, they were sterile after that. Today, in the

Land of Instant Gratification, we nuke just about every-thing. Remember, we Baby Boomers want it now.

9. The La-Z-Boy recliner – Every guy (you're sounding chauvinistic here, Mike) feels the primal need to own one or more La-Z-Boys. It is the unofficial chair of the NFL. **[Note to Publicist – Investigate the possibility of developing a line of La-Z-Boys in team colors and logos – End Note]** American men spend more time sleeping in a La-Z-Boy than in a bed. I made that up, but I'm pretty sure it is true. Maybe I should become a politician? Oops, sorry, it must be the wine talking.

The La-Z-Boy was invented by two furniture business owners in 1928 and was marketed as "nature's way of relaxing."

10. The bra, or brassiere as you Francophiles call it – You might say this is the foundation of civilization – OK, another bad analogy. Legend has it that the bra was invented by Dolly Parton, who fashioned a prototype from the material in a trampoline. It keeps "the girls" high and perky. Without the bra, there would be a lot of bruised kneecaps. I often think that if one of those straps were to break, it would knock down everyone within a five-foot radius.

Yes, I know I've had my Top 10, but there are several honorable mentions that I can't pass up.

11. Velcro – As the punsters say, "Stick with me, baby." How did we ever tie our sneakers before Velcro? According to Wikipedia, Swiss engineer George de Mestral

invented this fastener when, in 1941, he went for a walk in the woods and wondered why burdock seeds clung to his coat and dog. He discovered the burdock method could be turned into something useful. He patented it in 1955 and commercially introduced it in the late 1950s.

Sticky George coined the name *Velcro*, a portmanteau of the French words velour ("velvet") and crochet ("hook"), for his invention. Damn, doesn't Mr. Google make me sound smart? Velcro was heavily used in the space program to keep things from floating away in the weightlessness of space, such as Tang containers, false teeth, and Russian cosmonauts. It is primarily used today to fasten children's and old men's sneakers. On behalf of mankind everywhere, merci, George.

Oh, yeah. Did you notice another $10 word, portmanteau, which is a high-falutin way to say "blend"?

12. The vacuum bottle – This is the second smartest device next to Mr. Google. How does it know to keep hot things hot and cold things cold?

13. Viagra – Keep it up, buttercup! Mr. Happy is alive and well and living in The Villages.

14. Duct tape – aka as "200 mile per hour tape." It sticks. Duct tape is the go-to fixit tool of every redneck in America. It holds together cars, trucks, furniture, etc., and it can be used to "handcuff" those nosy revenuers.

15. A tie between the beer bottle (Where would we be today without a six-pack?) and the refrigerator. (How could you keep your six-pack cold?)

Okay, that's my Top 10+ Best Inventions of all time. Now let's move onto the Worst Inventions. What were these guys thinking?

Chapter 23:
Bottom 10 Worst Inventions

1. Taxes – Taxes are the root canal of your pocketbook. One wouldn't mind paying taxes if you got something for your money. With our dysfunctional government, it's like pouring money down a black hole, or a hole of any color, for that matter. P.S. If any IRS agents are reading this, remember, the positions expressed herein do not necessarily represent the views of the author. (I got this line from infomercials on TV where a station is protecting itself from lawsuits. I need to stay low from this agency's perspective.)

If taxes are the root canal of your wallet, then Congress are the dentures of government. They don't bite into their work, they give you a product that's hard to swallow, and they should be taken out and cleaned periodically. Just sayin'!

2. Birthday candles – Enough already! I don't need a cake and candles to make me feel old. I am old, and I feel it every day. Why risk a house fire to drive the point home?

3. Colonoscopy and prostate exams – Can you imagine the weird person who dreamed these up? The genius who invented the prostate exam must've said to his fellow doctors, "Hey, guess what? I'm going to stick my finger up this guy's butt and see how things are going." I bet

they laughed at him at their medical get-togethers and called him a pervert behind his back. Oh, yeah, and how did he talk the first patient into this procedure? Did the doctor have to get him drunk first? And did he call him the morning after?

The prostate exam is tame compared to a colonoscopy. Here's the basic process:

a. Drink 20 gallons of a bitter sludge that is mixed with flavors to mask the vileness (the masking doesn't work).

b. Sit on the toilet all night long while you cleanse yourself by shitting your brains out, and you reach the point where your butt is so sore from wiping that you can't sit no more.

c. Have your colon, intestines, and tonsils invaded by a 50-foot cable with a flashlight, camera, and Swiss Army Knife attached to the end. If polyps are detected, it's snip, snip, snip.

d. Listen to "Doctor Speak" of the results. The only part you understand and hear is that you will have to do it again in one, three, or five years.

Face it, the colonoscopy inventor makes Dr. Prostate look almost sane.

4. Computers and communication devices – Hold on a minute. I know you are thinking "This guy must be senile. He listed computers and communication devices in the Best 10 Inventions, and here he has them in the Worst 10? Too much wine?" Au contraire, mon frere (no way,

Jose). Although these tech marvels have tremendous benefits, they have some serious side effects – just like you see in medicine ads on TV which scare the bejesus out of you. On the downside:

a. Smart phones have created techno-zombies who always have their nose in the phone – while walking, during restaurant meals, on airplanes, etc. They are oblivious to the world and their companions.

b. The children of techno-zombies who spend every waking hour playing computer games.

c. The texters who communicate only in texts when a phone call would be quicker.

d. People who become prisoners of their phones. Maybe that's why they're called "cell" phones?

e. Artificial Intelligence, where the computer learns through experience and becomes more "intelligent." The danger here is if the computer should become more intelligent than humans, we could end up being their slaves, e.g., your Roomba 580 could have you cleaning the floors.

This reminds me of a quote I saw online: "Last night the internet stopped working so I spent a few hours with my family. They seem like good people."

5. Disco – Including the music, the clubs, the DJs, the dances, the dance contests, and the clothing. To all the John Travolta wannabes reading this – take off that

white bellbottom leisure suit and polyester shirt open to your navel, kiss the girl in the hot pants goodbye, and get back to reality. Disco was a sad phase in our musical history. Basically, the music was mindless and consumeristic. Although it was panned as a movement, there were several positives that came with it including the Bee Gees (loved the falsetto), the Village People (It's fun to stay at the YMCA), and the strobe lights and mirrored balls (crazy about those puppies).

6. The bathroom scale – If you look up "liar" in the dictionary, it will show a picture of the bathroom scale. I am fairly certain that this sucker creates increased weight readings to get you to diet. It's all part of an AMA conspiracy. I'd like to see the algorithm that the scale makers use to determine the fatty weight additions. Now that you know this, I'm sure you will ignore any number that the scale reports. (My guess is that 75% of you already do.)

7. Robocalls – May the people that do this spend eternity in Hell. Just as you sit down at the table or in front of the TV or in a lawn chair for a meal, you hear the ring a ding a ding of a robocall from a disguised number. The caller is a computer with a political message, a life insurance promotion, a hearing aid offer, or a funeral plot to sell. The "Do Not Call" list is ineffective in preventing the calls, and you can't vent your spleen because there ain't no one on the other end. But hope springs eternal. I think that I may have a solution here. Xfinity now offers a service called NOMOROBO that sends the call to Call Forward Heaven after one ring. It is like a phone bug-zapper – you hear one ring then silence. Another one bites the dust.

8. Commercial air travel – Good old Orville and Wilbur really created what has evolved into a travel monster here. First of all, most commercial planes are older than we are. Doesn't that give you a warm and fuzzy? Fortunately, the planes operate in a safe environment. It's not like they fly at thousands of feet above the ground, right? Second, the planes are designed by ex-sardine packers: the more bodies on the plane, the better for margins. Third, airline food is notoriously BAD. (Most airlines have fixed this by eliminating food – you can't screw up a bag of crackers and a Coke.) Next, the airlines operate on a "success schedule" – everything must go right for the system to work. Weather, mechanical delays, heavy air traffic, etc. ripple through the system and create delays that multiply. Then the flight attendants don't want to be on the flight any more than you do, and they don't try to hide it. In addition, carry-on storage is precious, and most of your fellow travelers have never heard of size limits. The restrooms are smaller than your luggage, and when you get up to go, the pilot turns on the "Fasten Seat Belts" sign for turbulence. And finally, you are usually seated (in the middle seat) beside:

   a. a passenger who requires the seat belt extender;

   b. a mother with a crying baby or a misbehaving kid;

   c. "Chatty Kathy" who talks to you the entire trip; or

   d. a snorer, farter or someone who skipped the shower today (maybe this week?).

9. Reality TV – Watching some group in a contrived situation getting voted off the island or seeking a bachelor/

bachelorette or dancing or spending 24 hours a day with them. Give me a good old colonoscopy any day. What ever happened to "Real TV" like *I Love Lucy, Andy Griffith, Laugh In,* etc.?

10. Alarm clock – This SOB never takes a break. Every weekday morning long before sunrise, it jolts you out of dreamland with 100 decibels of aural pain. I think the Devil invented it, or at a minimum, he sets the time. And in today's electronic world, you don't even need a clock. You can be disturbed by a smart phone, smart watch, tablet, Siri, Alexa, Google Hub, etc. Ain't technology wonderful?

Again, there are several honorable mentions that I can't leave out.

11. Emojis – The dumbing-down of America. I am not even going to go there.

12. Facebook – As detailed in Chapter 21: Change, I can't understand how people get joy from showing their meals before they eat them or want to advertise extended absences from home or discuss politics, religion, and biases with the world. I have seen a suggestion that has three Facebook buttons – "Like," "Dislike," and "Stop being stupid." This may be one direct way of giving your "friend" some "friendly" feedback.

13. Liver – Nobody should have to eat this shit.

Okay, that's the Bottom 10+ Worst Inventions ever.
So, given all these good and bad inventions, what

kind of things were put out to pasture in our lifetime, the buggy whips?

Chapter 24:
Buggy Whips

Just to make sure everyone is on the same page, you are on page _____ (fill in the blank).

Seriously, my definition of a buggy whip is a product which ceased to exist because the need for the product was eliminated, often by an invention. The namesake case was when the buggy whip industry was eliminated by the automobile. The following are my choices for Top 10 Buggy Whips:

1. Dictionaries and encyclopedias – Forget buying and carrying these boat anchors around. Mr. Google has kicked your butt. eBay is flooded with these dinosaurs.

2. The slide rule – Calculators, computers, and iPhones have made the slide rule redundant. Now the only ways you can identify an engineer are his pocket protector and white socks. He no longer wears a slide rule in a holster on his belt.

3. Dinner conversation – If you are seated at the kitchen table or if you go out to a restaurant, nobody talks to each other. Everybody's head is buried in their smart phone. If you need to communicate with someone in the room, you can always text them.

4. Gas station attendants – Let me get this straight. You want somebody to pump gas for you, check your oil, and wash your windshield? You gotta be kidding, Caveman.

5. Land lines and fax machines – There is no longer a need for them. Everybody has a smart phone which can do many times what a land line can do. You say you need a land line to connect your fax machine – what fax machine, Mr. Bell? Today's printers can scan documents for transmission in an email.

6. User Manuals – Tree huggers, rejoice. User manuals, quick guides, and setup instructions are all online. Of course, prehistoric creatures like me access them, print them out to read, and keep them in a file by habit.

7. Mom-and-Pop Stores – This is an unfortunate consequence of changes in the retail world. First it was the big box stores like Lowe's, Walmart, Home Depot, Best Buy, Dick's Sporting Goods, etc. that offered a vast array of merchandise in a large display facility (one-stop shopping). Then it was the bulk-buying, cost-cutting clubs like Costco and Sam's Club, who have expanded their offerings broadly over time. If you need 48 rolls of toilet paper or 500 multivitamins or 20 gallons of Tide, this is where you get it. And finally, the online stores like Amazon do away with the storefront and deliver to your door within one or two days, sometimes the same day. Amazon has created the ultimate in logistics. With Amazon delivery, it's like Christmas every day, opening boxes brought to you by the jolly old driver in his or her smiley-arrow-logo sleigh. You can also track your order in

real time and watch the delivery truck on a map driving down your street. Way cool!

By the way, if I were an evildoer, as characterized by George Dubbyah Bush, and I wanted to attack the US of A, I would dress my soldiers as Amazon delivery people and send them out in their smiley-arrow-logo vans filled with soldiers. They could penetrate neighborhoods and capture cities without discovery before it was too late. **[Note to Stephen King – Think about the idea. If you want to kick it around, call me. – End Note]**

My advice to struggling mom-and-pop stores is to start selling medical marijuana and CBD. This is a "growing" market and has a "high" profit, pardon the puns.

The next three buggy whips are technically not products that were eliminated by changes in technology. They are practices or facilities where technology has made them go away, or they are in the process of going away.

8. The driver's left foot – In days of old, the driver used his left foot for two important functions. First, he used it to control the high beams of his headlights. Now this function is accomplished via a stick on the steering column. Second, he used his left foot to engage the clutch and shift gears. Today the vast majority of cars have automatic transmissions, and if any shifting is involved, it is clutchless and done by paddles on the steering column. Now there are only two minor reasons to use the left foot. Many older drivers in Florida keep the left foot on the brake pedal and the right foot on the accelerator and drive with two feet. So when you are following them, their brake lights are constantly flashing on and off. Treat this as a warning signal: "Old Driver on Board

– Stay Back." The other minor use of the left foot is that some young drivers prop their left foot up on the dash to relax while driving. You think I'm kidding? Not! Treat this as a warning: "Stupid Driver on Board – Stay Back."

9. Offices – Today telework and telecommuting are reducing the need for office space. According to Global Workplace Analytics,[xii] regular work at home has a grown by 159% since 2005, more than 11 times faster than the rest of the work force; 40% more employers offered flexible workplace options than they did five years ago; 50% of the US workforce hold a job that is compatible with telework; and 80 to 90% of the US workforce say that they would like to telework. And studies show that office desks are now vacant 50% to 60% of the time.

Businesses would save an average of $11,000 per half-time telecommuter per year. The telecommuters would save between $2,000 and $7,000 a year. And the greenhouse-gas reduction would be equivalent to taking the entire New York State workforce permanently off the road.

Offices may never become a buggy whip, but they are certainly going to become less important in the work environment. More and more workers will be able to sit at home at their computer, in their underwear or PJs, and get their work accomplished (while multitasking by watching *Oprah* and *As the World Turns* on TV). Ain't technology wonderful?

10. Analog – An analog signal is a continuous sine wave that changes over a period of time. Numeric values are described by the amplitude or frequency, or phase. It has

no fixed range. A digital signal is a discrete square wave that carries information in binary form. It's either a one or a zero. Digital technology has essentially replaced analog signals. Think of it. Your TV has gone from analog to digital, your watch has gone from analog to digital, communication devices have gone from analog to digital, etc. I think we can all say goodbye to Mr. Analog.

So there you have it. My take on the Top 10+ Best Inventions, the Bottom 10+ Worst Inventions, and the 10 Buggy Whips created by technology.

Chapter 25:
Politics

Back in the good old days when Congress actually accomplished something (many of the readers are way too young to remember this), Tip O'Neill, the Speaker of the House, told us, "All politics is local." What he meant by this was that the politician must support his local constituency to be successful.

Well, the Tipper may have been right for his day, but for today, the model has changed to Life Lesson 84.

Life Lesson 84: All politics is loco!

Think about it, amigo. Today, once a politician is elected, his or her number-one job is to get reelected. Political parties are taking positions that are untenable. Our system has become dysfunctional. But as Ronald Reagan would say, "There you go again, Mike. You're getting too serious."

Let's suppose your son or daughter tells you, "I want to be a politician when I grow up." What can you do?

1. Hire an exorcist. This evil demon must be washed out of his or her system.

2. Change your name, move out of the country, and don't give them your new address. This is known as the BC maneuver, named for the dark-of-night

move the Baltimore Colts made to Indianapolis in 1984. (Did Orwell predict this coincidence?)

3. Apply for the Witness Protection Program.

4. Give them large doses of castor oil to flush their bowels.

We're talking serious doo-doo here, bucko. Politicians rank Number One (Yes, Numero Uno) on the Sleazy 100 Careers List.

Mark Twain said the following about school boards, but I think it is more appropriate for politicians.

Life Lesson 85: In the first place, God made idiots. That was for practice. Then he made politicians.

Chapter 26:
The Universal Law of
Population Segmentation
(The 5/95 Rule)

I believe that when dealing with people, everything in this world adheres to a fundamental law of population segmentation, which I have made Life Lesson 86.

Life Lesson 86: In a group of people, 5% of the population influence the performance for 95% of a group characteristic.

The basic form for this rule is "5% of (fill in the blank to describe a population) (fill in a verb) 95% of (fill in the blank to define a characteristic).

Let me give you some examples:

1. 5% of a manager's employees take up 95% of his or her time.

During my career I found this to be true. The 5% are constantly wanting feedback, promotions, whining, and causing workplace disturbances.

2. This was also true in my tenure as president of our condo's board of directors – 5% of the residents required

95% of my time, the board's time, and the staff's time. They only wanted "to help." They had numerous "suggestions." They pointed out things that they thought should be changed. And I soon found out that they would never be satisfied. Solve one problem or issue, and they moved on to the next.

3. How does this apply to getting things done? The 5/95 Rule in this case reads: 5% of the employees deliver 95% of the value. These are the keepers. Challenge them, reward them, and mentor them.

4. And what about our tax system? In this case, 5% of the taxpayers pay 95% of the revenues. OK, that's not exactly true. It's 68% of the revenues, but if you listen to several of the progressive Democrats, it could be 95% in a couple of years. Hold on there, Mr. Mike – no politicizing. Get back on track.

5. Since we just discussed politics, I will mention the 5/95 Rule for politicians: 5% of all politicians have an IQ above 95. Perhaps this explains their actions – and then again, maybe not.

6. And finally let me give you the ultimate example that we all face, which is Life Lesson 87.

Life Lesson 87: 5% of the people in any group are assholes 95% of the time.

Think about it. You may conclude that my numbers

are low. Unfortunately, the worldwide distribution of assholes is not even. For example, in the US, California, New York, and Washington, DC have disproportionately large numbers. Therefore, you may be in an "asshole-centric" area.

Now let's move on to PART V, which is MUSINGS.

PART V:
MUSINGS

Okay, I've retreated to my writer's cave with a bottle of Italian Chianti. Now it's time for deep reflection and thought. Meditation is in order, Swami. So let's get a little cognitive and abstract, free the mind to wander and ponder, pardner. To quote Matthew McConaughey in the *Dallas Buyers Club*, "All right, all right, all right!" Incidentally, the Queen has a thing for Matthew and even considered buying a Lincoln SUV after seeing his ad on TV. But once again, I digress.

If this part of the book seems more disconnected than the others, it is. That's what happens when you have been in the writer's cave too long, or you've been listening to the Beatles records played backwards, or you had some weird-tasting mushrooms with your tofu for dinner. Random thoughts burst into your consciousness, and you type like mad to capture them without spilling the Chianti. Here is a sampling of my wine flashes.

To start off, I will discuss my hobbies, what I do in my spare time for amusement. And because a person's music gives an insight into their soul, I'll discuss my musical tastes.

Then, since I provided a sample of my bucket list in PART I, I will share the total current list here. Next, I am a proud father and grandfather, but parenting ain't always easy. I will expound on children and grandchildren. And finally, I'll give my thoughts and experiences on giving back.

Chapter 27:
Hobbies

The online dictionary defines a hobby as an activity done regularly in one's leisure time for pleasure. This definition is rather broad and may lead to confusion. For example, I don't think your wife will buy "drinking beer" as a hobby. However, Betty White has noted, "Vodka is kind of a hobby," so maybe you can get away with it.

My definition of hobby is Life Lesson 88.

Life Lesson 88: A hobby is an expensive diversion.

Think about it. The only cheap hobbies are panhandling, playing checkers, and "shitting a tire." Otherwise, it's pay-to-play. Wait a minute, you say. What is "shitting a tire"?

When we were teenagers, new tires came wrapped in paper. One could create the same look by wrapping an old tire in toilet paper. However, before we did, we covered one sidewall with horse or cow manure. Then we wrapped it and placed it manure-side down along a deserted stretch of road. We waited in hiding until a driver came along thinking fortune was smiling on his new-found "treasure." He would open his trunk and grab the tire, only to become covered in Holstein doo-doo. That was the signal for us to run like hell, because a chase usually occurred. Remember, McConnellsburg, PA is a town of 1,200 people and two red lights. Excitement was hard to find.

You are probably familiar with what "They say" – "Don't look a gift horse in the mouth." Once again, I challenge "They." This activity is best summarized by fine-tuning the adage into Life Lesson 89.

Life Lesson 89: Don't put a gift "horse" tire in the trunk.

But my point is that most hobbies are expensive diversions. In fact (true story), I know a man whose hobbies are wine and golfing, so he bought a winery and a golf course in California. Now we're talking real money and expensive diversions!

I am like everyone else; I have my list of hobbies. And since retirement, I have the time to pursue them. Let me describe my diversions.

1. Cars

I mentioned earlier that I'm a Car Guy. I love automobiles. I enjoy having clean, fast, and undented rides. When I'm out shopping, dining, etc., I park my car out in Booneyland and walk. This is theoretically intended to prevent someone from banging their doors into my car. However, if you remember the 5/95 Rule, the 5% of the world's population who are assholes purposely pull up next to you, even though there are 25 spaces around you.

I also don't trust carwashes (this fear is called "scratchaphobia"), and I always wash and wax the car myself. And

I'm religious about getting the car serviced according to the manufacturer's schedule. When I trade in a car, whoever buys it gets a like-new vehicle.

Here's the list of cars that the Queen and I have owned.

A. 1939 Chevrolet Sedan – This was my first car, and it saw me through high school (and over the mountain to the exotic world of Chambersburg, PA).

B. 1955 Chevrolet Sedan with a Corvette engine and transmission – My brother and I shared this classic car during high school.

C. 1962 Sunbeam Alpine Convertible – This British sports car with four-speed transmission and overdrive was a chick magnet. I had this car during the first two years of college, and I was driving it when I received my only traffic ticket. It had straight-through mufflers, and when I took off from my fraternity, the State College cop heard me a block away. He flashed me down on a hill, and when he bent over to check out the underside of the car, his "Smokey the Bear" hat came off and rolled downhill on the brim. I laughed uncontrollably. Bad move. Here's the ticket, kid! This leads us to Life Lesson 90.

Life Lesson 90: Respect your elders, particularly those with a citation book in hand.

D. 1963 Corvette Stingray Convertible – This was the first year of the Stingray. I had the car during my junior and senior years in college and then after the Queen-To-Be and I got married. When we had our son, child car seats were not required or widely used, so we placed a small plastic baby seat between the car's bucket seats. This worked well until Todd was big enough to begin kicking the car out of gear with his feet, an indicator that it was either time to get a family car or to put the kid up for adoption. It was a tough decision, but I guess we did the right thing in selling the Vette.

E. 1968 Opel Kadett Rally –This was a beautiful gold and black five-speed, sporty German car that was powered by gerbils. Call me Mr. Family Man.

F. 1972 Lancia Sedan – You've probably never heard of a Lancia, but it was an Italian four-door, five-speed automobile. It was a beautiful car until I dropped a log on the fender while bringing in firewood from our garage. It cost me my Paul Bunyan merit badge from the Boy Scouts.

G. 1974 Fiat Spider Convertible and 1975 Oldsmobile Cutlass Coupe – The bright orange Spider pumpkin was my car, while Andrée purchased the Cutlass. The Olds served us well until the Queen, who was selling real estate at the time, had a client's kid throw up all over the back seat. Time to hang an air freshener from the mirror and trade in this baby.

H. 1968 Toyota Land Cruiser – I bought this used "box on wheels" as a fishing car. When it ran (which was a small percentage of the time), it was perfect for hauling half-kegs of beer to tailgates, etc.

I. 1978 Datsun 280 Z 2+2 Hatchback – A bright yellow car that was fast and pretty, like a flying banana.

J. 1981 Audi 100 Diesel –. The diesel fuel had a propensity to gum up when it got extremely cold outside. The answer was to spray volatile ether from a can into the air intake. We were in Vermont skiing in 1982 at the time the Air Florida plane froze up and crashed into the 14th Street Bridge on takeoff from National Airport in Washington, DC. The weather was extremely cold, and the Audi wouldn't start. The Austrian lady who ran the hostel where we were staying was sure that I would blow up her inn by using the spray, and every morning she was outside yelling at me, "Shoe are goink to blows up zee buildinks." I didn't. Her "buildinks" are still standing.

By the way, how cold was it? It was so cold that one of us got frostbite on his butt from riding the chairlift even though he was wearing long underwear and ski pants. Brass monkeys, beware!

K. 1982 Datsun Four Wheel Drive Pickup – C'mon, man. Every guy in America needs a four-wheel-drive pick-em-up. What a rust bucket. Show me a surface or a joint that wasn't eaten (or eating) away.

L. 1985 Mercedes 300 SD – The Queen bought this gihugic diesel "tank" for her real estate practice. Lots of space, but it weighed more than an 18-wheeler.

M. 1986 Subaru XT Turbo – This was a great little, fast, and economical five-speed. When Todd went to law school, we gave it to him and he used it, and abused it, through the years.

N. 1986 Porsche 914 Turbo – This was a great car and was a blast to drive. Unfortunately, I owned it in State College and could only drive it four or five months a year. So I sold it for a four-wheel-drive vehicle.

O. 1989 Jeep Grand Cherokee – A practical car for State College (and fishing).

P. Company cars – I had two Ford LTDs and a 1995 Chrysler Concorde, all big, heavy, roomy blobs – but you couldn't beat the price.

Q. 1991 Mercedes 300 Sedan – Again, this was a real estate car for the Queen. Business must have been good.

R. 1979 Mercedes 450 SL Convertible – The Queen purchased the two-door SL from my father, who had bought it new. This move celebrated her retirement from real estate and our relocation to Dallas. Big D – big hair – big red sports car. When our grandson was born, the Queen realized that the SL wouldn't accommodate a child's car seat. This was the second time we sold a car and kept a kid.

S. 2005 Corvette C5 Coupe – This was the first year of the C5. It had a removable top and a six-speed transmission. Raw power for crawling along, bumper to bumper on the Dallas tollway during rush hour.

T. 2009 BMW 530i Sedan – The Queen finally switched from Mercedes and went with the Beamer. This occurred about the time that I retired.

U. 2012 BMW X5 SUV–– I bought this car to be able to travel back and forth to our Pennsylvania fish camp. The Corvette just wouldn't handle the Queen's "necessities."

V. 2011 Honda Pilot – We wanted a car that I could use at the fish camp and then leave in Pennsylvania. Our intent was to buy a used Pilot, but the Queen decided she didn't want a "vehicle that somebody else had used," so we bought a new one.

W. 2012 BMW 535i Sedan – A Queen needs to stay current, right?

X. 2015 Audi Q7 Diesel – This was a great car for traveling, and the diesel got tremendous mileage, but this was one of the cars that was caught up in the Volkswagen gas mileage scandal. As a result of VW/Audi trying to calm the waters with "loyalty" packages and the VW settlement suit, I received a prepaid $500 Visa card, an Audi gift card for service and merchandise worth $500, a $9,500 settlement check, and a $1,000 final check when the emissions fix was installed. The total of $11,500 meant that I drove the car for three years (without any problems) for free. Thank you, VW cheaters.

Y. 2014 BMW 640i Convertible – The current Queen-mobile.

Z. 2017 Honda Pilot Elite – This was a replacement car for the 2011 Honda Pilot. There was nothing wrong with the 2011, but the Queen decided it didn't have all the bells and whistles that she wanted. The 2017 does!

A. 2018 Audi Q7 – This is my current baby. It's an all-black (black optic package) car, and it has every option you can get. With no chrome, it looks like a Mennonite hearse. When the seats are down, it has 70 ft.^{3} of space, big enough to haul a casket. It has almost enough room for the Queen's traveling necessities. With the seats up, it accommodates six – pseu-do-comfortably.

It's a good thing that the list has ended because, as you may have noticed, I ran out of alphabet and was starting over.

The uninitiated reader could look at this list and say, "You sure have pissed away a lot of money on cars." That is heresy to a Car Guy. As Françoise "Frenchy" Sagan put it, "Money may not buy happiness, but I'd rather cry in a Jaguar than on a bus."

Remember the friend who bought the winery and the golf course? He's also a Car Guy, and he has something like a nine-car garage in his house filled with red exotic cars, including an Aston Martin DBS and a Ford GT. A hobby is just a hobby until there's real money involved; then it's a passion.

2. Motorcycles

In addition to automobiles, I also made a hobby out of motorcycles. In the early '90s, I bought a used Kawasaki 650 to see if I still enjoyed riding (I had a small Ducati when I was growing up). I called my dad and said, "Guess what? I bought a motorcycle." His response was "I hoped you had grown beyond that stage." He also asked me, "What do they think about it?" I said, "Who is they?" and he replied, "Well, Raytheon, of course. Don't they care if you kill yourself?" I told him I didn't know because I hadn't asked.

I really enjoyed the Kawasaki, so I bought a used Harley Dyna Wide Glide, and I ended up taking this bike to Texas.

Shortly after I bought the Harley, the Queen surprised me by secretly taking the motorcycle safety course and getting her motorcycle license. When she came home and showed it to me, I said, "Does this mean you want to motorcycle of your own?" Her response was "No. I just thought something might happen to you and I would need to know how to ride." I said, "What the hell are you gonna do, strap me across the saddlebags and drag me home?" The Queen never used her motorcycle driver's license, but she sure was proud to have the biker stamp on it.

After we went to Texas, I purchased a new Harley Road King Classic. This was a great bike, and we spent many Sundays in our leathers, cruising the backroads of Texas and terrorizing the locals. (OK, I'm embellishing things, but maybe we scared a stray dog or two.) I enjoyed it until we moved to Florida where the unpredictable, erratic, ancient drivers convinced me to sell it.

3. Fly Fishing

Fly fishing for trout is a passion of mine. I was taught by a friend and colleague at work when I was in my early 20s, and I've been trying to master it for the last 50 years. As Izaak Walton, the author of *The Compleat Angler*, wrote in 1653, "As no man is born an artist, so no man is born an angler," and Theodore Gordon, the father of American dry fly fishing wrote, "The great charm of fly-fishing is that we are always learning."

Every April, I spend time in central Pennsylvania fly fishing for trout. When I was working, I would take a week off to fish. I did that for 42 years. Upon retirement, the week became five weeks.

Let's talk theory and reality. In theory, the time between mid-April and early June is primo for northeastern US fly fishing with great insect hatches on the water. Reality has shown that for the last ten years, the weather during this period has been "sucky," a fishing term for cold, raining, and even snowing. The creeks and rivers get "blown out," swollen over their banks and brown like a chocolate milkshake. So why do I keep coming back early? Tradition and the hope of theory actually occurring. Damn, I love the sport!

When we moved to Florida, I decided I needed a fish camp in Pennsylvania. The Queen and I had two different ideas about what a fish camp was. My concept was a cabin on the water far away from everyone else. I guess you can say that this did not go over well with the Queen. In fact, that's a gross understatement. She told me where I could put my cabin on the water. She wanted to be in town, near grocery stores, restaurants, hairstylists, and people. Eventually we compromised and bought a townhouse in Boalsburg, Pennsylvania, near grocery stores, restaurants, hairstylists, and people. The "fish camp" has three bedrooms, three bathrooms, kitchen, dining room, living room, laundry room, and one upstairs family room where I am actually allowed to display fishing stuff. I realize it's not a real fish camp because we don't have any dead animals hanging on the wall, but I'm working on it.

On the positive side, since the Queen won't come up to Pennsylvania until it's warmer. I have two to three weeks of solace until her Grand Arrival in early May.

For a trout fisherman, State College, Pennsylvania is ideal. I shouldn't be telling you this because I don't want it to get overcrowded (or more overcrowded than it already is), but within 45 minutes of State College, there are a dozen trout streams. Now, I can count on you to keep the secret between us, right?

When I was younger, I was on the stream at daylight and finished at dusk. Now that I have matured, the hours have shortened, and the pace has slowed. With my Parkinson's, I have trouble keeping my balance when wading on the rocky, slippery streams, so I use a wading stick and don't go in many places I used to fish.

When I want to relax, I go out fishing and unwind in a serene setting. I have discovered Life Lesson 91.

Life Lesson 91: Trout hang out in beautiful places.

They aren't like catfish or carp that reside in some muddy hole filled with trash and probably dead bodies. This leads to a derivative of a Zane Grey quote which is Life Lesson 92.

Life Lesson 92: If one fishes only to capture fish, his fishing trips would have ended long ago.

The beauty of it is the beauty of it – silence, rippling water rushing around you, watching the fish rise to feed, casting a fly to seduce one to take it, and sometimes successfully catching and releasing it back into the waters.

I say sometimes because trout are picky (they don't just take any old fly floating by), and they are always on guard. Think about it. The size of a trout's brain is about the size of a pea. On the other hand, the average human brain is three pounds, and it is six inches long. Intuitively, the fisherman should win the battle more often. But the trout has more at stake.

Remember, if you rearrange the letters in TROUTER, which is someone who fishes for trout, it spells TORTURE, and that just about sums it up.

4. Puzzles

I am a card-carrying member of Puzzleholics Anonymous. The first step for recovery is to admit that I am
powerless over puzzles and my life is unmanageable. It
all started out so innocently. I have degrees in Math and
Computer Science, and I really enjoy logical challenges.
I began by working Sudoku and crossword puzzles, and
I advanced through the *New York Times* and the *Wall
Street Journal* weekend crossword puzzles. Then I got
hooked on cryptic puzzles where each clue is a puzzle in
itself, e.g., "Headless Dog and Bird," and the answer is
EAGLE (beagle minus the b), or where the answer must
be altered before entering, e.g., each square in the dia-
gram must contain either zero or two letters.

There are variations such as acrostic puzzles, rows
garden, etc. I like the cryptic puzzles in the *Weekend
Wall Street Journal*. Rather than wait for the Saturday
paper delivery, the WSJ posts the puzzle around 4:15 PM
Eastern time on Friday. I print it and am lost to the world
until I have solved it (sometime between Friday night
and Tuesday/Wednesday). During that time, there is an
occasional "Mike sighting" by the Queen, but basically, I
become invisible.

The good news regarding my addiction is that since I
started writing this book, I am not spending my free time
doing puzzles. A breakthrough? No, I'm spending my
free time writing the book. I'm still a ghost in the house.
Maybe I should join Authorholics Anonymous?

5. Golf

I love golf. I hate golf.

You think I'm strange saying this? Well, I'll guarantee you that 98% of all golfers say the same thing. When you nail a drive or sink a long putt, you love the sport. When you shank the ball off into the woods or miss a one-foot putt, you despise the damn game.

Unfortunately, I didn't take up the game until later in life. During my career, it was difficult to find five hours of time to play 18 holes. After we retired, the Queen was looking for things we could do together, and she suggested we take up golf. I thought this would be a flash in the pan for her – buy the equipment, take some lessons, buy a dozen golf outfits, and move on to the next Royal idea. Wrong! Wrong! Wrong!

We did all that with the clothes, clubs, and lessons, and she became hooked on the game. She joined a women's golf league. She took enough lessons from the local pro that he was able to buy a new Cadillac and house and put three kids through college. She was a fanatic.

I have to admit it was a good suggestion from the standpoint of doing things together. We spend many a day (that's an old person's saying) golfing as a twosome or in a foursome, enjoying a lunch afterward and relaxing.

As you might expect, the Queen is the best-dressed golfer on the course. She really looks the part. And that's as it should be.

We joined the Longboat Key Club and made many new good friends as a result. We play in monthly scrambles and have dinner afterwards. Who says you can't have fun when you're old?

By the way, two years ago the Queen completely surprised me by coming home carrying a huge trophy cup. She and her partner had won a ladies' member-guest tournament at the Longboat Key Club. Of course, this was facilitated by one word – "handicap." The handicap system is designed to put everyone on an equal footing, and this time it worked. So here I am tonight, sitting in our office, staring at her member-guest trophy and gritting my teeth.

6. Boating

I've done a lot of dumb things in my life, but I've never owned a boat. When we lived in Annapolis, Maryland, our friends had a boat. We provided the beer and the food, and they provided the boat. Brother, we got off cheap.

Everyone knows that any boat is an expensive undertaking. When you buy one, your first thought is: "I just added another thing to the What The Hell Was I Thinking List."

So now I am faced with a moral dilemma. Our new house has a boat dock and lift. And it looks lonely. Is God giving me a sign, like he did to Noah, with the dock/lift? Should I buy a boat?

To date, when visitors see the dock and ask: "Do you have a boat?" I tell them yes, but it's at the marina for servicing. Everyone believes this because typically a boat is at the marina for servicing 82% of the time. But eventually everyone will catch on.

The salt air, sun, heat, and humidity are tough on a boat. And the marinas' services are legendary with respect to cost. A friend of mine told me that everything is measured in "boat units." When I inquired what a "boat unit" is, he explained, "If you take a boat in for service, the minimum charge is $1,000. So $1,000 is a boat unit."

Subconsciously, I have probably decided already to get a boat, so I bought the Bible on boating, *Chapman Piloting & Seamanship*. It is 950 pages and weighs 200 pounds. If you don't use it for boating information, you can always use it for weight training.

7. Retiree Hobbies

Lest we forget, all retirees share another set of hobbies – doctors' visits, shopping and lunch at Costco, early bird suppers, and managing their pills.

Now that we're musing right along, let's take on music, which provides insight into the soul. (OK, that's a groaner of a pun – sorry.)

Chapter 28:
Music

In his magnum opus (stilted words meaning "master-piece"), the German philosopher Arthur Schopenhauer wrote, "It has always been said that music is the language of feeling and passion, as words are the language of reason."

Right on! Tell it like it is, Dr. Artie! Can I get an Amen? Ok, let's dissect this hyperbole.

1. This occurred in 1818 when learned professors used stilted language to prove their smartiness.

2. Arthur "Eloquent Artie" lectured at the University of Berlin, but his course was cancelled due to poor attendance. (Do you think his language had anything to do with it?)

But let's see if we can stay focused on the message for a moment. It's simple – you are what you listen to!

I have a confession to make. My two favorite kinds of music are country and western. Dave Barry, I hope you can forgive me. I grew up on rock 'n' roll. As a Baby Boomer, who didn't? But in the mid-1970s, I made the transition to the outlaw country music of Waylon, Willie, and the boys. At that time rock 'n' roll was evolving into the heavy-metal genre (French for 'shit'), and I found that country music was understandable and conveyed messages about real life (even though it might be the real life of miscreants).

What do I like about country music?

1. When you listen to country music, it makes you feel good. I don't mean the misery story that the singer is relating, but the fact that you are in a hell of a lot better shape than he or she is.

2. Country music always tells a story, e. g., about a love gone bad, about a drinking problem, about falling in love head over heels, about America, about a cowboy's life, etc. Contrast this with "Who let the dogs out?" or "Beat it."

3. I love to hear a fiddle play.

When I say country music, I'm talking about real country. I mean Willie Nelson, Waylon Jennings, George Jones, Garth Brooks, Meryl Haggard, Alan Jackson, Toby Keith, Loretta Lynn, Reba McEntire, David Allen Coe, Robert Earl Kean, etc. There are currently a number of pretenders out there claiming to be country singers. This is a technopop illusion called "country pop." Don't call Carrie Underwood or Luke Bryan or Taylor Swift a country singer.

Is there a perfect country song?

David Allen Coe sings about one in his rendition of "(You Don't Have to Call Me Darling, Darling) You Never Even

Called Me By My Name." He tells about his friend Steve Goodman who wrote this song, and how Steve believed it was the perfect country and western song. But it was missing something. He tells it and sings it this way:

(Spoken)

Well, a friend of mine named Steve Goodman wrote
    that song
And he told me it was the perfect country & western
    song
I wrote him back a letter and I told him it was not
    the perfect country & western song
Because he hadn't said anything at all about mama
Or trains, or trucks, or prison, or gettin' drunk
Well, he sat down and wrote another verse to the
    song and he sent it to me
And after reading it I realized that my friend had
    written the perfect country & western song
And I felt obliged to include it on this album
The last verse goes like this here:

(Sung)

Well, I was drunk the day my mom got out of prison
And I went to pick her up in the rain
But before I could get to the station in my pickup
    truck
She got run over by a damned old train

Now you gotta admit, pardner, that is sweet. It has my vote for the perfect country song.

Country Music Lyrics

I am also fascinated by the topics of the C&W songs, particularly the titles, which are often frank and colorful. I am not making these up (all you Missourians, go ahead, check them out):

    A. You're the Reason Our Kids are Ugly
    B. Up Against the Wall Redneck Mother
    C. (You're Hotter Than a) Three Peckered Goat
    D. I'm at Home Getting Hammered (While She's Out Getting Nailed)
    E. She Got the Goldmine (I Got the Shaft)
    F. Dropkick Me Jesus (Through the Goal Posts of Life)
    G. Here's a Quarter (Call Someone Who Cares)
    H. My Give A Damn's Busted
    I. Save a Horse (Ride a Cowboy)
    J. Queen of My Double-Wide Trailer
    K. Why Don't We Get Drunk and Screw
    L. If That Ain't Country (I'll Kiss Your Ass)
    M. The King is Gone (So Are You)

Now picture this. Every Saturday night, the little woman and I put on our jeans and boots, get in our Ford F150 with a gun rack in back, turn on Sirius Radio to Channel 60, Outlaw Country, and cruise around Geezerville, looking for a honky-tonk. Just jerking your chain. I drive a Dodge Ram truck, not a Ford.

While I'm confessing my likes and dislikes in music, I need to come clean on several outliers. I still listen regularly to the Beatles, the Rolling Stones (particularly when

I'm working out), the Bee Gees, and Neil Diamond, so I'm not a one-trick pony, but rather, I'm quite multicultural.

So there you have a summary of my present and past hobbies.

Chapter 29:
The Bucket List

"Bucket List" is the term that was coined for the movie of the same title in 2007. It is a list of things you want to do before you die, i.e., kick the bucket. At my age of 74, it wouldn't be prudent to have a bucket list that is too long (or to buy green bananas, as is frequently said), and I need to be careful that the items are things I know a septuagenarian can do. Septuagenarian is another $10 word that is worth the price of this book. No, it is not an astrological sign or an organized religion; it is a person between 70 and 79. For your information and continued education, septuagenarian is followed by octogenarian (80-89), nonagenarian (90-99), and centenarian (100-109). Anyone older than that is called George Burns. George had sage advice about living: "If you live to be one hundred, you've got it made. Very few people die past that age." But I am wandering again. So let's get back to the topic, and let me give you a look at my current list.

1. Write a memoir to pass along life lessons, etc., that I have gathered over time and to share the potpourri of random thoughts that inhabit my mind. OK, I'm on my way to crossing off this item. By my updated calculations, I'm only months from completion.

2. Attend a Rolling Stones concert before Sir Mick

reaches the age of 100, or is married for the 100th time, or has his 100th child – whichever comes first. How does the man do it? Raw energy. The original Energizer Bunny. I get tired just watching him. By the way, I'm pretty sure the other members of the band died, and Mick had them stuffed by a taxidermist and controls them like puppets. Just watch them closely next time and see if you don't agree.

3. Break 90 for 18 holes of golf.

4. Have lunch with Dave Barry at a Hooters. This would be a two-fer bucket list item for me – lunch with Dave Barry and going to a Hooters. **[Note to Dave – Dave, if you are a regular patron of Hooters, I'm sure we could find another haute cuisine place for lunch. Also, I am aware that you're living in Colorado now in the Witness Protection Program, so I could meet you at a clandestine place of your choosing. I would be happy to wear a disguise if you think it is necessary. Please have your people contact my people to set it up. I am using the cover name "Mark Twain." – End Note]**

5. Take another Great American Road Trip and fish the west. Plans are being developed to make 2021 the year for The Great American Road Trip III.

6. Visit Alaska. In Chapter 18, Travel, I talked about a short business (system deployment) trip to Adak, Alaska, but I would like to go back on a pleasure trip. Given the Queen's aversion to cold, this is a

low-probability item, somewhere between "Hell No" and "Are you friggin crazy?"

[Note to Readers – Recognizing that I need to remain alive to complete these bucket-list items, I have decided to forgo an earlier item – running with the bulls in Pamplona. I am considering modifying it to be "walking with the heifers in Pennsylvania." – End Note]

Chapter 30:
Children and Grandchildren

Let me begin by stating Life Lesson 93.

Life Lesson 93: The primary purpose of having children is to have grandchildren.

Well, OK, maybe the exceptions to this are farmers who need their kids' help in the fields and Social Security scammers who need the extra income.

I don't mean to sound harsh. I love my son. But let's be honest. Children from birth until 12 are a lot of work – feeding, training, cleaning up after, chauffeuring, and the list goes on. It's a full-time job. And children between the ages of 13 and their early 20s are a pain in the butt. They live in a world of their own, they are emotional (hormonal), and their parents don't know anything (or as they might say, "Don't know Jack Shit"). Hopefully, after the early 20s, they recognize reality and the parents become much smarter. The problem here is proximity – you are together all day, every day.

Our son, the teenager, was no different. He knew it all. And we were the strictest, most old-fashioned parents in the world. If we said black, he said white.

During his senior year in high school, I said to him, "You have three choices – you can go to college and we'll pay your way, but you're moving out of the house. You can go in the service, and you're moving out of the house. Or you can get a job, and you're moving out of the house." Have you picked up on the theme here? The next week my wife got a call from the Marine recruiter in Harrisburg, Pennsylvania. He said that because our son was underage, he needed our permission to take the Marine Corps physical. The Queen went batshit (and beyond). When we asked him about this, he said, "I really want to go to college, but I figured I needed a back-up plan."

Todd went to college, Penn State, and graduated with a BA in Political Science. Then he went to law school and graduated from the California Western School of Law.

It is amazing how the Queen and I became so much smarter between the time he was 16 years old and the time he was 25 years old. We must've been taking IQ pills.

And the relationship has continued to grow. We are extremely proud of the man he has become.

I think Charles Wadsworth, the pianist, said it best in what I state as Life Lesson 94.

Life Lesson 94: By the time a man realizes that maybe his father was right, he usually has a son who thinks he is wrong.

Ain't turnabout poetic justice?

The Queen and I have two wonderful grandchildren whom we love dearly. Holden is 19 and a freshman at Clemson University (still a tough pill to swallow for Mr. Penn State). Claire is 16 and a sophomore at the Rivers

School, a private school in Massachusetts. Both are out-standing students, excellent athletes, and nice kids. And we are spoiling them as all grandparents do.

Again, it's a matter of proximity. We only spend time with them periodically, and they are great during these visits.

Even if they felt we weren't smart, they would never say anything. This is the difference between children and grandchildren. Yeah.

Now I move on from Children and Grandchildren with one final Life Lesson, which is a derivative of a R.D. Laing quote.

Life Lesson 95: Children are a sexually transmitted disease.

Chapter 31:
Giving Back

The Queen and I are very fortunate. We have lived a comfortable life, had fulfilling careers, developed lifelong friends, traveled extensively, and enjoyed ourselves. But not everyone is as favored. And we believe that we should try to make a difference where we can. One place where help is needed is in changing the landscape for at-risk children and families living in our community. We have found an organization, Children First, which serves over 700 at-risk children, from birth to five years old, and their families in Sarasota County. The majority of the families served are below the Federal Poverty Level.

Poverty disrupts a child's education, development, and growth and is the single best predictor of a child's failure to achieve in school. Children First provides services to both the child and the family to ensure development physically, emotionally, socially, and cognitively, and to prepare them for kindergarten. Additionally, the children are provided a healthy breakfast, lunch, and snack which accounts for over 50% of their weekly nutrition.

Children First is funded by the Federal Government's Early Head Start (birth to age three) and Head Start (ages 3 to 5) programs and by philanthropic contributions. Children First has been a Head Start national Program of Excellence (top 1% of 1,800 programs) for the past four years.

OK, so how could we help?

Bait the Hook and Reel Them In

We were introduced to Children First by our realtor Jo, and we began to support the organization financially. The Queen also helped on various committees in support of fundraisers. Then in 2015, while we were having Christmas dinner with Jo, her husband, and several other couples, and after I had had two glasses of wine, she asked me, "Have you ever considered volunteering at Children First?" This evoked a quick and firm "NO," brief and to the point. Then she went to Plan B and asked me, "Well, would you consider visiting Children First and seeing what occurs in the classroom?" Remember I've already had two glasses of wine. So I agreed (Mr. Congeniality), and she set up a visit. When I got to the classroom, filled with about fifteen four to five-year old children, I was impressed. I had anticipated the focus would be on learning, but I hadn't realized the development opportunities for social interaction, hygiene, physical exercise, communication skills development, problem solving, and the healthy meals. It is a well-rounded, comprehensive approach. And the energy coming from these four to five-year old kids was contagious. Therefore, I left the room agreeing to become a volunteer teacher (actually a teacher's aide in the classroom). From then on, I spend my Tuesday mornings as Mr. Mike, helping out in the Blue Crayon room. The job responsibilities are broad, i.e., do what the teachers ask me to do. This includes helping set up for activities, reading to the children, tying shoe-laces, pushing swings, and semi-controlling the physical energy released on the playground. When was the last time you played with Lincoln logs? Or with crayons? Or finger paints? Well, I do it regularly.

When I walk into the classroom on Tuesday mornings I am greeted with "Good morning, Mr. Mike." This adds joy to the day. Approximately 75% of the children have a single parent, often a single mother, and they welcome the addition of a male father figure (OK, grandfather figure, or more likely great-grandfather figure).

And children between the ages of three and five say what they think. It's often amusing and sometimes sad. For example:

1. One little boy, Allen, said to me, "Mr. Mike, do you have a girlfriend?" I said, "No, Allen, I'm married," and he responded, "But don't you have a girlfriend too?" I found out later that Allen's dad had both a wife and a girlfriend.

2. And Romero asked me, "Mr. Mike, why do you have a mustache?" I said, "Romero, it makes me look distinguished." And he said, "It makes you look like a penguin." Took the wind out of my sails, but maybe he was right.

3. The children have a bathroom in the classroom, and one day Amir was on the throne with the door open. I said, "Amir, close the door," and he said, "I can't, Mr. Mike, I'm poopin'." Right again.

4. During an activity session, Marie came up to me and

said, "Mr. Mike, you've got something in your nose. I'll get you a tissue." She gave me a tissue and I wiped my nose and asked, "Marie, did I get it?" She shook her head no, so I wiped my nose again and asked, "Now did I get it?" She said, "Yes, Mr. Mike, now go wash your hands." The hygiene lessons are working.

5. When I asked one little girl a question, she said, "My mother told me not to talk to any white men." I said, "Fine, I respect that," and we went about doing other things. Later that morning, the two of us were playing and chatting together with no preconceived perceptions. This is an example of learning and environment.

I could go on with things that I learn each week, but I'll summarize with Life Lesson 96.

Life Lesson 96: When you give, you get.

There is great satisfaction in believing that you are making a difference in the future for these children and families. And when I leave on Tuesday mornings and hear "Goodbye, Mr. Mike, we love you," I feel good.

Does It End There? No! No! A thousand times no!

The CEO and President of Children First is a charismatic leader, and we have become friends over the years. Unfortunately, he has me on speed-dial, and when he needs something, it's like Ghostbusters – who ya gonna call? Mr. Mike.

To date, he has asked me to be on the board and multiple committees of the board, for Andrée and me to co-chair several fund-raising galas, and to be the board's liaison with the Policy Council, a group of parent representatives from the thirteen Children First locations in Sarasota County. And I have been honored to accept. I am currently serving as the Chair of the Children First Board of Directors.

If only I could figure out how to get the darn Do Not Call thingie to work for the CEO's phone number.

Now, let me summarize where this writing experiment has taken us.

PART VI: SUMMARY (WE MADE IT!)

Congratulations to you and to me. We both lasted through the ordeal, which is no small feat. Permit me to summarize my undertaking in terms of Objectives Satisfaction, Statistics, The Path Forward, The Future, Thanks and Credits.

Objectives Satisfaction

When we started out, I posed the question "Why Am I Writing This Book?" and I listed five reasons:

1. I am 74 years old, and I have lived in a period of accelerating change. I now have the time to look back and reflect on all this, and I'd like to pass on some of what I have learned as Life Lessons.

2. I have never written a book. It is on my bucket list.

3. Over the last eleven years, my wife and I have enjoyed extensive travel, and I have chronicled our adventures in a series of blogs which have resulted in feedback that was positive and made me believe that I had a story to tell.

4. I am a closet comedian. I love to tell stories and make people laugh. This is my attempt to come out of the closet. Peek-a-boo!

5. Time is not on my side. Get-Er-Done while I'm still on the sunny side of the sod.

Well, as the French say, "Fait accompli, mon ami and amiette." I Got-Er-Done.

My objective was to write a humorous self-help book where the self-help Lessons Learned aren't arcane or theoretical in nature, but rather, they are practical and street smart. I will leave it to the reader to judge how well this was done.

I really hope that you got a few laughs from my experiences and that you have enjoyed the ride. Looking back has been fun for me.

If you are weird enough to want to use parts of this material in your non-commercial writing, speeches, marriage vows, curses, etc., please feel free to "steal shamelessly." I would be flattered. Just spell my name correctly, please. Any commercial use requires prior approval per copyright.

Finally, I trust that you have found the free definitions of esoteric, novel, unusual, au courant $10 words to be educational, and I hope they are useful in your conversations and writing, or even when you are dissing someone, e.g., "Your momma is a procrastinator who turns tricks for septuagenarians." See if your adversary has a response for that!

Statistics

Remember, I am an engineer, and engineers love numbers, so here are a few statistics on the process and the product.

1. Writing Time – It took me five months to go from commitment to a complete draft and another two months for editing and polishing the draft and having a manuscript evaluation done. This is much shorter than I calculated (and feared) early in the process. The wine "acceleration" regimen made the difference.

2. Length – The book contains approximately 55,000 words. This meets my self-imposed ideal length for a self-help memoir.

3. Life Lessons – I generated 98 Life Lessons, and I hope there are some ponies in here for you among all the horseshit.

4. Writing Regimen – I used eleven cases of Costco red wine (Cabernet, Malbec, Chianti, and Rioja) to prevent writer's block and make the words flow. My tax returns will capture this expense for supplies, as well as the retroactive eleven years of travel expenses for the Post-Retirement Travel chapters of the book. **[Note to CPA – We're counting on you to come through with a favorable interpretation here, Mr. Loopholes – End Note]** I understand that the IRS likes round numbers to make their calculations easier, so I will round up both the bottle count and price as the basis for

the expense. By the way, I am shopping for a new sports car to help create the successful image that an author deserves. **[Note to Dave Barry – DB, any suggestions? – End Note]**

The Path Forward

Once again, I have reached the point where, as a novice, I need a path forward. This is a euphemism for "I'm lost again, bucko." What do I do now? I will continue to use my assistant, Mr. Google, and I have also engaged Booknook.biz to provide editing services, cover design, and the self-publishing products required for both eBooks and Print on Demand books, By the way, if you are reading this, it means that either I was successful, i.e., the book was published, or you hacked into my computer. Either way, thanks for the interest.

The Future

As the Eyetalians say, "Que sera, sera," which means "Beats the shit outta me." Whatever the future holds, I'm not going to change it, but I intend to tackle it "full ass."

I plan to face the future challenges with Life Lesson 97.

Life Lesson 97: Keep your pecker up and your powder dry.

Hey, don't cringe and gasp out there in Readerland. "Keep your pecker up" is a British expression that means stay positive, and "keep your powder dry" means be cautious and prepared. Leave it up to those crazy Brits to be colorful in their communication.

As I looked back, I asked myself if I would do anything differently with my life if I got a Mulligan (a golfing term for score improvement, also known as a Do-Over), and my bottom line is not as far as the big picture is concerned. I am comfortable with the fact I did it my way.

"And now, the end is near..."

I am in the fourth quarter of the game of life, sports fans. The game summary to date is:

1. I've lived a life that's full – Actually, in consonance with Life Lesson 37, I've lived a life that's full-ass, not half-ass;

2. I've had a few regrets – They really are too few to mention (well, there was that weekend in Tijuana with the Fiera twins and also not buying Apple stock when it came out);

3. I've met the challenges - Sometimes I bit off more than I could chew, but I faced it all. For example, "Hey! Let's write a book. How hard can it be?";

4. I've had a variety of emotions – I've loved, I've laughed and cried as a result of my 53 WONDERFUL years being married to the Queen; and

    I did in fact do it my way!
    My parting advice to you is:

1. Be humble – Heaven knows we all have a wealth of reasons to be so.

2. Make fun of yourself – Beat the others to the punch.

3. Strive to make a difference – Whether it is giving back or doing your best or trying to make the world a better place, be a driver and not a passenger. It is so much more rewarding.

4. Have fun – As Mark Twain said, "Humor is mankind's greatest blessing."

Incidentally, for the curious readers – when I told you that I was writing this book under the nom de plume of Samuel Clemens, that wasn't a random selection. Samuel Clemens was Mark Twain's given name. But you erudite bibliophiles probably knew that.

Thanks and Credits

I owe a special thanks to the Queen, my life partner during 53 WONDERFUL years of marital blitz – typo, I mean "bliss." She has continually:

1. Developed this poor old country boy through his career and retirement years by her innate mentoring skills as a counselor, advice-giver, doctor (diagnosing medical issues and suggesting treatments), critic (perhaps her Numero Uno forte), coach, back seat driver, and haberdasher. To hear her speak, she must have about 50 honorary PhDs from the best colleges in the nation.

2. Been an exceptionally good sport about my

incessant, sometimes brutal, embellished writing about "the Queen." She knows that I love her and that I am doing this for effect. Don't get out the super glue yet, sweetheart.

3. Accepted my prolonged absence from the real world while writing this book.

I want to repeat a Life Lesson on how I feel.

Life Lesson 33: When you have a Queen, don't reshuffle the deck and end up with a Joker.

And let me add the final Life Lesson 98.

Life Lesson 98: It doesn't matter where you're going, it's who you have beside you.

Love you, babe.

I also want to thank my assistant Mr. Google and Lady YouTube for the research that went into the book. Wikipedia also provided considerable material on cities and towns, medical conditions, demographics, marriage statistics, etc. And after exhausting these resources, I just made stuff up. (Just screwing with you to check your attention level.)

And a special thanks in advance to Dave Barry for his kind words about my book, which I know will be forthcoming. **[Note to Dave – Call me and we will do lunch. – End Note]**

A Final Note

My writing muscles are tired. When I started this journey, I did not appreciate the amount of effort that goes into a book. But I am glad that I did it. Cross one item off the bucket list.

Thanks to all of you who have joined me in this journey.

Mike

Endnotes

[i] Claire, Amy. "Who is They? It's Time to unmask that know-it-all" http://www.chicagonow.com/armchair-cook/2016/03/who-is-they-its-time-to-unmask-that-know-it-all. 3/21/2016

[ii] Malatesta, Mark. "Book Genre Definitions – Book Genre Dictionary" http://www.book-genres.com/genres-of-books/book-genre-definitions/.

[iii] Reddgari, Manasa. "10 Big-Ticket Tax Deductions for Writers." *MileIQ.* https://mileiq.com/blog/10-big-ticket-tax-deductions-writers/amp/.

[iv] Han, Seunggu, MD. "Essential Tremor" http://www.healthline.com/health/essential-tremor. 11/29/2017

[v] Wikipedia. "Parkinson's Disease" http://www.wikipedia.org/wiki/Parkinson's_disease.

[vi] Banschick, Mark MD. "The High Failure Rate of Second and Third Marriages" https://www.psychologytoday.com/us/blog/the-intelligent-divorce/201202/the-high-failure-rate-second-and-third-marriages

[vii] Specktor, Brandon. "Marriage Statistics: The Biggest Surprises About Love, Sex, and More" http://www.rd.com/advice/relationships/marriage-statistics-the-biggest-surprises-about-love-sex-and-more.

[viii] AreaVibes. "Longboat Key, FL Demographics" http://www.areavibes.com/longboat+key-fl/demographics.

[ix] AreaVibes. "The Villages, FL Demographics" http://www.areavibes.com/the+villages-fl/demographics.

[x] Broadway, James M. "Why Does Time Seem To Speed Up With Age?" – *Scientific American* https://www.scientificamerican.com/article/why-does-time-seem-to-speed-up-with-age/

[xi] Gaiam. "7 Health Benefits Of Laughter" http://www.gaiam.com/blogs/discover/7-health-benefits-of-laughter.

[xii] Global Workplace Analytics. "Latest Telecommuting/Mobile Work/Remote Work Statistics" http://www.globalworkplaceanalytics.com/telecommuting-statistics. Updated August 16, 2019.

Made in the USA
Columbia, SC
21 March 2021

34826047R00152